Lesson planning for effective learning

Lesson planning for effective learning

Martin Fautley and Jonathan Savage

 Open University Press

Open University Press
McGraw-Hill Education
McGraw-Hill House
Shoppenhangers Road
Maidenhead
Berkshire
England
SL6 2QL

email: enquiries@openup.co.uk
world wide web: www.openup.co.uk

and Two Penn Plaza, New York, NY 10121–2289, USA

First published 2013

A catalogue record of this book is available from the British Library

ISBN–13: 978–0–33–524690–8 (pb)
ISBN–10: 0–33–524690–7 (pb)
eISBN: 978–0–33–524691–5

Library of Congress Cataloging-in-Publication Data
CIP data applied for

Typesetting and e-book compilations by
RefineCatch Limited, Bungay, Suffolk

Printed and bound by CPI Group (UK) Ltd, Croydon, CR0 4YY

Fictitious names of companies, products, people, characters and/or data that may be used herein (in case studies or in examples) are not intended to represent any real individual, company, product or event.

Praise for this book

"This is essential reading for all teachers, teacher educators and policy makers. For new entrants to the profession, it offers the opportunity to think beyond the notion of folk pedagogies and to consider how a more powerful theoretical framework might underpin lesson planning. It presents essential analysis as to why common approaches to teaching and learning have emerged and become embedded – this provides a great opportunity for more experienced teachers to develop a deeper critical understanding of their practice. Punctuated with reflective questions, it enables the reader to reconceptualise planning and pedagogy and to engage in theorised reflection on practice."

Kate Laurence, Institute of Education, University of London, UK

"At last! A plain speaking book on effective lesson planning.
Lesson Planning for Effective Learning by Martin Fautley and Jonathan Savage combines theoretical perspectives with really useful, instantly useable examples from everyday practice. Despite the scholarly approach, the 200 pages of this little book retain an essentially conversational quality ensuring that it is equally accessible to students, academics and learning enthusiasts alike."

Andrew R. Mackereth, Headteacher, Heart of England School

"Lesson planning is one of the most fundamental duties of teachers no matter what their subject, age phase or experience. In their latest book, Martin Fautley and Jonathan Savage start with practice and, in deconstructing what teachers do every day, apply their deep thinking and reasoned consideration. They are adept at weaving a wide range of thoughts, experiences and theory into the mix, making this readily accessible and ultimately a very helpful book.

Martin and Jonathan make much of the novice-expert continuum. I'm not sure where I fit but I certainly experienced a number of 'penny-dropping' moments that immediately led me to reflect and sharpen up my own planning. I've been reminded of the huge complexities that there are in planning effective lessons, both the "private preparation and the public performance" elements. It is impossible to read very far into this book without realising that planning for effective learning has little to do with the administrative task of completing a planning pro forma, important and necessary though *that is. This book makes it abundantly clear that pedagogy and pedagogical content knowledge underpin planning for effective learning. Although, as the authors point out, much lesson planning is invisible, what they do so well here, in the words of Russell and Loughran*, is to "make the tacit explicit". Above all, this book articulates something of what it is to be professional for teachers of all types. I heartily recommend this book."*

Simon Spencer, Birmingham City University, UK

* Russell, T. & Loughran, J. (2007) *Enacting a Pedagogy of Teacher Education: Values, Relationships and Practices*, London: Routledge

"This book gives fantastic insight and practical strategies for teachers at all points within their career in order to encourage and embed reflective practice. For outstanding practitioners and senior leaders, it provides case studies and examples which will stimulate discussion and provide starting points from which to develop policy at whole school level, and influence and develop practice at an individual teacher level. A 'must have' resource for any school Teaching and Learning Group library."

Hayley McDonagh, Senior Leader, Golden Hillock School, Birmingham. Former LA senior adviser working with Schools in Ofsted Category

Contents

Figures

Tables

Acknowledgements

We would like to extend our thanks to our families, friends and colleagues at both Birmingham City University and Manchester Metropolitan University, who have supported our work and read various extracts for this book as it has been prepared. We are also grateful to all our colleagues teaching in schools, who have given their time and shared their thinking with us as we worked on this book. We are very grateful to all of you for your help and assistance.

We would also like to thank Simon Spencer of BCU, for his thinking concerning lesson planning, and on being able to include a BCU plan as an example. Our thanks too go to Hayley McDonagh and Suzanne Jerkins, who have helped with providing examples of documentation, and of sharing with us ways in which schools approach lesson planning.

And finally thanks to all of our students, who continually challenge our thinking (in a good way!), and whose search for ever-improving lesson plans has helped us shape our own thinking.

Martin Fautley
Jonathan Savage

Introduction

Welcome to this book on lesson planning! We trust that you will find it a useful exploration of the key ideas related to planning an effective lesson. Whatever age of pupils you are teaching, or whatever subject you are teaching, learning to write clear and concise lesson planning is an essential and integral part of being an effective teacher. Throughout this book we will be arguing that there is a clear link between the mainly private mental and physical preparation of writing a lesson plan, and the public delivery of that plan through your teaching of a particular class. The essential link between that private preparation and public performance is your pedagogy. Therefore, much of our time in this book will be spent defining and exploring this link.

This book is designed in two parts. Part 1 contains a general exploration of the main elements of lesson planning and how they relate to your classroom pedagogy. In Part 2 we will explore some more general themes and ideas and relate these to the key issues discussed in Part 1.

Following this introduction, Chapter 1 introduces the common components of lesson planning. These include discrete elements such as learning objectives, learning outcomes, starters, teaching activities and plenaries as well as broader strategies such as those associated with differentiation, personalization and assessment. Right at the outset, we will be considering aspects of teaching 'style' and your role in bringing these basic elements to life within your teaching.

Chapter 2 focuses in on the lesson plan document itself, asking key questions about what it can and cannot do. There is a myth that the perfect lesson plan will ensure good lessons. We want to show that the thinking behind a lesson plan is more important than the lesson plan itself. We discuss what lessons plans will and will not do. A common misconception, for example, is that lesson plans need to involve hours of planning details down to the last minute. We will point out that reflexive teaching cannot by its very nature be that prescriptive. We will deal with common pitfalls faced by both novice and experienced teachers alike, including time management, over- and under-running, optimum learning time and activity sequencing.

Chapter 3 continues this theme by considering a range of practical pedagogical strategies by which your lesson plan can be 'brought to life' through your teaching. It introduces a simple triangle of interrelated activities (planning, pedagogy and reflective practice) through which your work as a teacher will develop. Drawing on key ideas from the work of Stenhouse and others, it asserts the notion that there is no meaningful curriculum development without teacher development. In other words, the quality of your lesson planning processes will have a direct influence on your own development as a teacher. The two are intrinsically linked.

Chapter 4 focuses on resources. It starts with ideas drawn from the concept of activity theory through which a discussion about how you choose and use specific resources will be framed. We will consider how positive approaches to the use of common resources such as interactive whiteboards and other pieces of technology can be developed before moving onto a broader exploration of different models of learning and how these are facilitated through the resources that teachers choose to adopt.

Chapter 5 turns our attention away from resources to individual pupils themselves. It explores how you can use the pedagogical strategies of differentiation and personalization to provide for educational needs of individual pupils. We will argue that all teachers teach 'mixed ability' classes and need focused strategies to turn broad lesson planning statements into meaningful classroom interactions with pupils, including those with challenging educational needs.

This chapter marks the end of the first part of this book, and Part 2 goes on to examine some broader themes and ideas and relate these to the key points raised throughout Part 1.

Chapter 6 opens Part 2 with a broad investigation into metaphors for lesson planning that draws on the work of Robin Alexander and others. Within it, we will be considering the notion of teaching as performance through a metaphorical reflection on the work of artists, musicians and footballers! This chapter will frame some of the broader ideas that we will discuss in the later chapters of the book including, in Chapter 7, those associated with learning. As we know, learning is a complex process. Knowledge is often seen as the outcome of learning, and yet knowledge itself is not unproblematic either. We know about a number of different types of knowledge, and this chapter deals with different types of knowledge that the teacher will meet, including the obvious types (declarative, procedural, acquisitive and participatory) as well as more complex types, such as tacit knowledge and pedagogical content knowledge.

Chapter 8 focuses on assessment. We will explore the differing purposes and uses of summative and formative assessment, and will emphasize that true assessment for learning (AfL) is an interactive process. Planning for AfL needs to be reflexive (and reflective – a point picked up in the next chapter) and involves a series of 'feedback loops'; pedagogy, within this model, can be helpfully conceptualized as a spiral with elements of feedback and 'feed-forward' informing it throughout. Assessment of learning (A of L) is also discussed here. Chapter 9 examines some similar themes within the context of medium- and longer-term curriculum planning. Recent legislation, and the rise of academies and free schools, have released many teachers from what some saw as the strictures of the National Curriculum. For all teachers there is considerable latitude, especially in Key Stages 1–3, concerning the content and organization of what is taught. The notion of curriculum mapping is important here, so in this chapter we consider how the teacher's broader planning can link with that across the school in a joined-up fashion, with topics and content planned for across subject domains with cross-curricular learning as an integral part of the overall planning routine.

Chapters 10 and 11 present a range of lesson planning documentation and materials drawn from the work of various teachers within primary and secondary schools. While it is not the purpose of this book to present a single document that you should use in your own planning, there are important lessons to be drawn from the work of other teachers. These chapters will present some common approaches with an accompanying narrative that reflects on these plans in light of the ideas discussed throughout the book. Our final chapter, Chapter 12, draws together key themes from throughout the book and, hopefully, sets you on your way towards a more skilful and informed approach to planning exciting, interactive and meaningful lessons for your pupils.

PART 1

1 Common components of a lesson

When discussing lesson planning it has become customary to talk about the component parts of a lesson. You will probably be familiar with many, if not all of these terminologies. To begin this chapter we need to spend some time deconstructing these component parts in order to be very precise in the language we are using, as there is not necessarily clarity of the terms employed across all users. Phrases such as 'the three-part lesson', 'aims and objectives', 'starters', 'plenaries', and 'mini-plenaries' are to be found throughout both the literature and the discourse concerning lesson planning, and knowing precisely what is meant by each can be challenging for novice and experienced teachers alike. This chapter discusses these alongside a number of other common components of a lesson, and explains not only what the terminologies mean, but why they are of use to teachers in both planning for learning and bringing that learning to life in the reality of the taught lesson in the classroom.

Let us begin by considering the format of the lesson itself. At its simplest, a lesson probably looks something like that shown in Figure 1.1. This simple lesson outline consisting of a beginning, a middle and an end may seem obvious, but let us consider what this means from both teaching *and* learning perspectives. The start of a lesson in many schools often involves a change: of rooms, of teacher, of subject, possibly of buildings. The opening of the lesson needs to take account of these, all of which can be considered as *variables*. You will

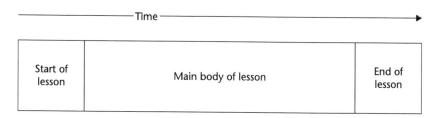

Figure 1.1 Simple lesson outline.

know whether the lesson happens, say, directly after break or lunchtime. These may well cause issues; if learners are coming in from outside, they may not all arrive together, they may be excited, wet, hot, cold, or many other things! This affects how you begin the lesson. Often there are routine admin matters to attend to, maybe you are required to take a register, or there might be notices to give out. From here you proceed to the main body of the lesson when the main teaching and learning activities will take place. The lesson ends with some form of summing-up, and of packing away, ready for an orderly end and dismissal.

This simple description of a lesson forms the basis of what has become known as the 'three-part lesson'. A three-part lesson follows the plan as described above, but with the constituent parts relabelled, as shown in Figure 1.2. Here the opening part of the lesson has been renamed 'starter' and there then follows the main body of the lesson as before. The final part of the lesson is now the 'plenary'. In this renamed version, the outside edges, the starter and plenary, assume a somewhat greater significance than in Figure 1.1. They are more than mechanistic 'get ready' or 'pack away' moments; they now form part of an integrated teaching and learning system in their own right. Let us consider each in turn.

Starters

The idea of a starter section is that it should be more than the routine admin-based procedure described above. A good starter should normally involve active learning and is designed to be an essential component of the lesson. As with the description of the beginning of a lesson in the simple lesson outlined above, it is important for the teacher to know whether all the pupils will be arriving simultaneously or whether there will be a staggered start if learners are coming from different preceding lessons, or from a break. The type of starter planned needs to take account of this, as a planned activity for all will be held up if the teacher and those pupils who have arrived are having to wait. This means that we can immediately categorize starters into two essential types:

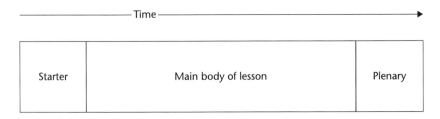

Figure 1.2   The three-part lesson.

1   starters for all, where the whole class is involved from the outset;
2   staggered starters, which allow for participation from late arrivals.

Knowing the type of starter required is the first stage in planning for it. From this follows planning for the content of the starter. It may be a stand-alone activity, it may act as a warm-up for the main body of teaching and learning to follow, or it may be a way of preparing the learners for what is to follow. It can also be appropriate at times to think of the starter as a behaviour management tool, as it may be needed to stimulate or calm down the learners from whatever they have been doing previously. Experienced teachers not only plan starters specific to the lesson they will be teaching, but also have a range of starters to use on special occasions when there is an unforeseen need not to do what was planned. These can be 'calm-down' starters, 'wake-up' starters, or very long staggered starters. It is worth the beginning teacher spending some time planning for these 'emergency' starters too.

Plenaries

The word 'plenary' comes from Latin, and means 'full'. The plenary can be viewed, therefore, as the part of the lesson which completes the teaching and learning experience for that session. The plenary is an important part of the lesson, but is one which many new and beginning teachers sometimes struggle to fit into the taught lesson (as opposed to the planned one!). There is an important bit of staffroom lore to the effect of 'pupils learn nothing once the bell has gone'. There is more than a grain of truth in this. Not only do they learn little, but there is also a professional responsibility to colleagues who do not want pupils to be late to their lesson any more than you do. Neither will you want your next class to be waiting if you over-run. But most importantly, you, the teacher, are in charge of your lesson and you should not let things get so out of hand that you allow the lesson to over-run and are taken by surprise when the bell goes. We will have more to say about the differences between the *planned lesson* and the *delivered lesson* throughout this book, but for the moment let us emphasize the importance of timekeeping!

The role of the plenary, then, is to bring to a conclusion the learning that has taken place during the lesson. This could take the form of a question and answer session, it could involve a reprise of key learning items, it could entail a sharing of work or activity that has been undertaken, it might involve a performance or a demonstration by selected learners, or it could involve learners recapping on what has been done. Allowing time for a plenary is clearly important, as it enables reflection and consolidation to occur.

Although we have described the plenary as happening at the end of the lesson here, it is important to note that this is not the only point at which it can occur. It can also be located at points during the lesson where reflection and consolidation would be appropriate. These plenaries can be referred to as within-lesson, mini-plenaries or ongoing plenaries. They are used to 'complete' (from the Latin!) the learning and activity that have taken place up to that point.

Aims and objectives

So far we have been considering the nature of teaching and learning from the perspective of the structure of the lesson. Before we continue any further, though, it is appropriate to think about *what* it is that you, the teacher, are going to be teaching, and importantly, *why* you are going to be teaching it. In order to begin to address these issues, we will now turn to a consideration of aims and objectives. These are often bundled together, as we have done here, but are rather different in both character and style, and should really be considered separately.

Aims

A lesson aim is concerned with the intentionality of the lesson. The aim of a lesson can therefore also be thought of as its purpose, and as the teacher planning the lesson it can be helpful to ask yourself '*why* am I teaching this lesson?'. The aim, therefore, is a general statement of intent. Here are some examples:

- The aim of this lesson is to introduce the learners to the concept of *pointillism* in art.
- Aim: To learn about Venn diagrams.
- Aim: To discuss the significance of the storm scene in Chapter 37 of *Far from the Madding Crowd*.
- The aim of the lesson is to improve accuracy when taking 'free kicks' in football.

All of these work as aims for the lessons in question. What they lack, however, is specificity concerning the teaching and learning that will be taking place in the lesson. This is the role of the objective.

Objectives

A lesson objective places the more philosophical aim of the lesson into a specific context. Objectives refer directly to what will be taught and learned in the lesson. Objectives are often encountered in groups rather than singly; whereas it is the case that a lesson will often have only one aim, it is entirely normal for the same lesson to have multiple objectives. Many schools still use the examples for learning objectives provided by the then DfES back in 2004 for this purpose:

By the end of the lesson pupils will:
- know that . . . (knowledge: factual information, e.g. names, places, symbols, formulae, events)
- develop/be able to . . . (skills: using knowledge, applying techniques, analysing information, etc.)
- understand how/why . . . (understanding: concepts, reasons, effects, principles, processes, etc.)
- develop/be aware of . . . (attitudes and values: empathy, caring, sensitivity towards social issues, feelings, moral issues, etc.)

(DfES/QCA 2004: 28)

These examples can be used as stems from which to construct objectives that focus attention onto the key reason for the lesson, namely *learning*. Objectives for learning can also be referred to as 'intended learning statements', 'planned learning', 'lesson objectives' or a variety of other titles. The important thing about them all, though, is that they refer to *learning*; this is learning, as opposed to *doing*. It is much simpler to write task objectives than learning objectives so this needs to be central in your mind as you think about the lesson. It should not be about what the pupils will *do*, but what they will *learn*. Certainly pupils will need activities in order to put their learning into action, but the lesson should not start from an activity with the learning tacked on as an afterthought, instead learning should be the very central purpose of the lesson in the first place.

It is for this reason, the difference between *doing* and *learning,* that it can be helpful for the teacher to differentiate for themselves the intended learning that they have planned for, and the way that this can be communicated to the pupils. Many schools require learning objectives to be shared with pupils at the start of a lesson, often written up on the board. Whether or not this is always good practice is open to debate, but given that so many schools seem to require it, distinguishing between 'grown-up' intended learning statements that you will have planned for, and child-friendly objective statements that you share with the pupils can be appropriate. Indeed, writing the text for those to share with the pupils can enable you to legitimately convert intended learning statements into task statements in ways that the pupils will understand. Doing this requires a little bit of extra thought on your part, but it does mean that you can be more effective in the way you plan for learning and activity to take place in your classroom.

Teaching and learning objectives

Although we have said that the principal purpose of the lesson is learning, it is clearly the case that in order for learning to flourish, teaching has to be appropriate to the subject matter in hand, and to the type and nature of the pupils in the class for the lesson. For these reasons, among many others, it is logical for you to think about the sort of teaching you will be doing in order to facilitate the learning you are devising in the lesson plan.

Learning objectives will detail learning, but it is highly likely that within the class there will be a range of abilities, of prior knowledge, of prior experiences and of understanding. This will be the case in all classes, even those which are ostensibly streamed or setted, and will be even more so in mixed-ability groupings, as we discuss later in the book. So teaching objectives could include ways of ensuring that all pupils in the class participate in the learning activities of the lesson in ways which are appropriate to their own personalized requirements. Such general objectives may well be common to a variety of lessons, but it is also desirable to think about detailed ones for individual lessons. This means that teaching objectives, based on the specific learning objectives illustrated above, might include such areas as:

- involving all the class in question and answer sessions, not just those with their hands up;
- ensuring that all pupils get a go at taking a free kick, not just the keen ones;
- choosing random pupils to demonstrate on the whiteboard what an overlapping Venn diagram entails;
- ensuring all pupils produce a piece of work which demonstrates their understanding of *pointillist* techniques.

These are specific teaching objectives, as we have said, other more general ones will be included too.

This discussion of learning and teaching objectives takes us into thinking not only about the content, but also the execution of the main body section of the lesson, and so let us now turn our attention to that area.

Episodes within a lesson

We have so far in this chapter dealt with what might be termed the 'edges' of the lesson, the starter and the plenary. The main body of the lesson will be where the majority of learning takes place so we need to deconstruct this in terms of what its common components might be, and of what planning for this section should entail.

It is important for all teachers, whether beginning or more experienced, to give considerable thought to the main section of the lesson. In order to start to do this, it is useful to break this down into a series of episodes, each of which has its own characteristics, but which when put together make up a coherent whole. There is no single magic formula for this – it will depend on a number of factors, including:

- the constituency of the class: top set, bottom set, mixed ability;
- the nature of the topic being taught: practical, theoretical, conceptual, skills;
- the availability of specialist equipment;
- the day of the week: would a difficult new topic be best addressed early in the week, rather than last thing on a Friday afternoon?
- the time of day: are mornings better peak learning time? Is the lesson just after the post-lunch dip?
- the weather(!): have they just come in from walking to school in a downpour? Is it windy? Is it snowing for the first time this year? (If so, forget it, with some classes!)

All of these can have an effect on learning, and although some can be planned for, as we say throughout this book, a good teacher is one who knows when to go off-script with their lesson plans and react accordingly and appropriately to whatever school life throws up that day.

But what can be addressed, and what should be planned for, is a sequence of teaching and learning episodes in which the teacher has deconstructed the required learning into a series of smaller steps. This is not just good practice in terms of providing variety, it also accords with what we know about how the brain learns:

> During a learning episode, we remember best that which comes first, second best that which comes last, and least that which comes just past the middle . . . The first items of new information are within the working memory's functional capacity so they command our attention, and are likely to be retained in semantic memory. The later information, however, exceeds the capacity and is lost. As the learning episode concludes, items in working memory are sorted or chunked to allow for additional processing of the arriving final items, which are likely held in immediate memory unless further rehearsed.
>
> (Sousa 2001: 88)

So, what should go into episodes within a lesson? Here there is a wide range of potential learning activities, tasks, ways of organizing pupils, and of facilitating learning.

Planning for learning episodes

You may be wondering at this stage why we are not simply telling you what the teaching and learning and learning episodes in your lesson should consist of. We know that:

> Many [beginning teachers] see teaching as an uncomplicated act of telling students what to learn . . . Consequently beginning teachers may enter pre-service programs with an expectation that they can be told how to teach and therefore appear to be in search of a recipe for teaching.
>
> (Berry 2008: 64)

Sadly there is no such 'recipe'! And in a similar vein there is no such thing as the perfect lesson plan. We are instead concentrating on getting you to think about what the components of your lesson should be and how to organize thinking about them in a logical way. To recap on what we have said so far, planning for learning episodes:

- needs to take into account a number of factors;
- should be class-/lesson-specific;
- should involve the teacher and pupils in different types of activity at different stages;
- should emphasize learning, not activity;
- should be focused on learning which derives from teaching.

So what sort of learning episodes should you be planning for? Clearly the answer to this question depends on the lesson! Typical activities undertaken by pupils in the classroom include those shown in Table 1.1:

This is not meant to be exclusive; there are many more activities which could be included. But it is meant to provide a basis upon which you can develop your own planning. A useful task you can undertake is to consider which learning episodes that would be appropriate for your context are not in this list.

Fitting all of these into a single lesson may prove demanding, but the purpose of Table 1.1 is to make you think about the sorts of learning episodes which you could include in a lesson. This means that you need to think about what is to be learned, and the sequence in which it needs to be learned.

Table 1.1 Typical learning episodes

Problem-solving	Discussing	Thinking
Practising	Rehearsing	Performing
Skill acquisition	Skill development	Teamwork
Making things	Creative work	Divergent thinking
Drawing	Remembering	Worksheets
Writing	Reading	Listening
Speaking	Communicating	Valuing
Forming opinions	Analysing	Experimenting

Teaching styles

The notion of episodes within the main body of the lesson takes us towards a consideration of the role of the teacher, not only in planning for learning to take place, but in what the teacher actually does during these episodes. One of the common tools used to describe this is that of the Mosston and Ashworth taxonomy of teaching styles (Mosston and Ashworth 2002; also in Leask 2009). This delineates a range of approaches to teaching and learning viewed from the perspective of the interaction and involvement of the teacher. It is shown in Table 1.2.

As you move through different episodes within a lesson it is extremely likely that you will also be moving between different teaching styles. This taxonomy allows you to plan for the different ways you can interact with pupils during these episodes.

Planning for sequencing learning

A lot of the thinking that goes into lesson planning is invisible, as are many aspects of pedagogy, but in planning a lesson you need to give a lot of thought

Table 1.2   Mosston and Ashworth taxonomy

Mosston and Ashworth teaching style	Meaning
Command	Teacher-centred, 'chalk and talk'
Practice	Teacher sets tasks for learners to practise
Reciprocal	Pupils work in pairs, one gives feedback to the other
Self-check	Teacher establishes success criteria, pupils work at own level against these
Inclusion	Teacher sets range of tasks, pupils choose which they wish to work on (*NB slightly different from usual usage*)
Guided discovery	Teacher guides the learner towards a predetermined outcome using questions and tasks
Convergent discovery	One outcome required, teacher guides (if necessary)
Divergent discovery	Many outcomes possible, teacher supports (if necessary)
Learner-designed	Teacher decides topic area, learner chooses own programme of study within this
Learner-initiated	Learner decides what they wish to learn, and organizes how they will do it
Self-teach	Entirely independent with no teacher participation

Source: Adapted from (Mosston and Ashworth 2002)

to sequencing learning episodes. For example, if you want to teach a child to play chess, you need to begin by explaining the point of the game, what winning entails, and then how each of the pieces moves. To do this you will need to sequence the information you give, it cannot come out in one great torrent of facts! You will also want the learner to have some experience of playing chess games in order to try out the moves they have learned, being corrected as they go along, and building up their confidence so that they can move towards mastery. Later on the child can think about tactics and forward planning, but in the early stages just getting the moves right is probably sufficient. Now, transfer the way that chess was being taught here to thinking about lesson planning. The sequence gone through is shown in Figure 1.3, where lesson planning activity is shown on the left, and the chess learning sequence on the right. This is clearly a rather over-simplistic view, but it does give an idea of one possible way in which planning for learning can be approached.

Let us take a closer look at the middle section of the lesson, viewed from the planning perspective, and think a little more about what is going on there. The section we are concentrating on is shown in Figure 1.4. This renders a very complex process such that it looks very simple – it is not! The notion of breaking down an activity into a series of stages is actually quite complex. Our chess example was comparatively straightforward, but suppose that the subject of the lesson was the Battle of Hastings? Or photosynthesis? Or any of a number of complex learning constructs that you will have to deal with? In these cases the breaking down into a series is much more complex, so how do you know where to start? And what do the pupils need to know in order to move on to the next stage? Some of these decisions relate to longer-term planning issues, a point we consider in Chapter 9. But what of the order within a lesson? To start with, it is helpful to think of what you want the pupils to accomplish in a single lesson, and work towards that. Then work out what the logical sequencing of knowledge should be. If they need to know *x* before they can do *y*, then this is fairly clear. If there seems to be a myriad of ways that the learning could be organized, then you could seek advice from other teachers, but you might wish to try your own sequence. If you teach in a secondary school, where you have multiple classes doing the same topic, you can try to vary the pattern between classes to see how they differ. The important thing is to have thought about the sequence beforehand, and know how you will do it.

In the simple chess example above we varied *instruction* with *practice*. The pupils learned how the pieces move, then had a go. Of course, you will want to use visual aids, the whiteboard, animations, and all the assistance of ICT with the instruction component here. But however you do it, you will then want the pupils to have a go themselves. One useful question you can ask yourself is:

> What is the minimum amount of information/instruction that the pupils need before they can have a go themselves?

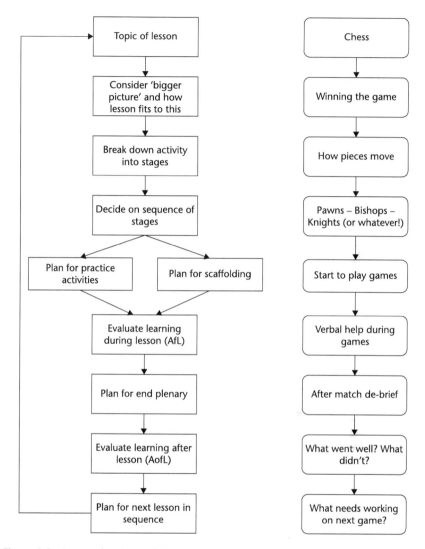

Figure 1.3 Lesson planning and chess.

Many beginning and inexperienced teachers make the mistake of talking far too much. Another common error committed by teachers is to explain exceptions too early on (a point we return to in Chapter 4). This will not help the pupils at the beginning. (To return to chess, if they have not yet mastered the game, there is little point teaching them about castling.) In practical subjects especially, the learners want to get on and have a go, so think about the minimum required information. Then having provided this, what comes next?

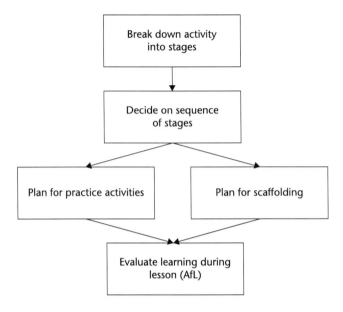

Figure 1.4   Planning for sequencing section.

Learning episodes and behaviour management

What comes next will obviously depend on what came before! But what many teachers like to do is to think about behaviour management at the same time as they plan for learning episodes. A well-planned lesson can go a long way towards alleviating behaviour management issues and the converse is certainly true: a badly planned lesson can cause behaviour management issues. So think back to the activities in Table 1.2. If you have just had a practical pupil-centred episode, do you want to follow this with a non-practical teacher-focused episode? If so, what is the best way of sequencing these into your overall lesson plan? It is also worth considering having mini-plenaries within an extended period of practical work, as not only will this help ensure that attention is focused in the right areas, but it will also help with behaviour management in that you will be able to rein in any untoward behaviour which may be starting to occur.

Bloom's taxonomy

Bloom's taxonomy (Bloom 1956) is well known among teachers in English-speaking countries. It places cognitive activity into a hierarchical list of thinking, with lower-order thinking at the base level, leading to higher-order thinking at the top. The normal order of these in Bloom's original taxonomy is shown on the left of Figure 1.5. Possibly of more use to today's teachers are the revisions which were made to the taxonomy by Anderson *et al.* in 2001. These revisions are shown on the right of Figure 1.5. The change from nouns to verbs is clearly helpful for the classroom teacher, but other points to note are the removal of synthesis as a category, the slight demotion of evaluation, and the new top-level category of creating. But what is particularly helpful is the overlaying of the new taxonomy with knowledge types. Learning theory, which we return to later in this book, categorizes knowledge into a number of different types, of which four are used by Anderson *et al.* These are shown in Table 1.3.

What Anderson *et al.* do is then to overlay these knowledge types onto the taxonomy to produce a grid as shown in Table 1.4.

Using this grid it becomes possible for teachers to place thought develop-ment and planning for both higher-order thinking and the important aspects of knowledge which need to be remembered at the heart of their planning. As some schools require Bloom's taxonomy to be explicitly referenced in plan-ning documentation, using this grid allows for different knowledge types to be mapped against higher- and lower-order thinking skills.

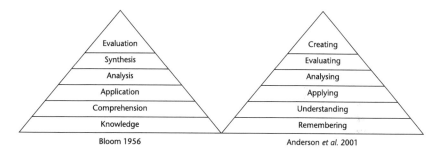

Figure 1.5   Bloom's taxonomy and Anderson *et al.*'s revision.

Table 1.3   Knowledge types

Factual knowledge	knowing learned facts, e.g. Paris is the capital of France
Conceptual knowledge	knowledge of interrelationships between things, e.g. knowing how to undertake long division when presented with a situation which requires it ·
Procedural knowledge	knowing how to do something, e.g. play the piano, or ride a bike
Meta-cognitive knowledge	knowledge of your own thinking, e.g. knowing that mnemonics may be helpful, or that imaging can help you remember

Table 1.4 Bloom revision and knowledge types

The Knowledge Dimension	The Cognitive Process Dimension					
	Remember	Understand	Apply	Analyze	Evaluate	Create
Factual knowledge						
Conceptual knowledge						
Procedural knowledge						
Meta-cognitive knowledge						

Source: From Anderson *et al.* (2001: 28)

Another place where Bloom's taxonomy is often invoked is in planning for questioning, and the way we have described it above gives some cues as to how it could be used. But let us first give some more detailed thought to questions and questioning.

Planning for questioning

We have seen the importance of planning for learning and of sequencing episodes within a lesson but there is another aspect of planning for learning which it is worth giving consideration to, and this is the area of *questioning*. We have already said that much planning is invisible in its execution, and the notion of planning for questioning may seem odd, but good questioning can really help to take learning forwards. As Ofsted observed: 'Success . . . is all about planning and preparation of the outline structure of the lesson, the teaching episodes, the questions to be asked and when they are to be posed' (Ofsted 2012: 4).

Planning for the questions that will be asked may seem one of those areas which teachers do spontaneously. But asking *good* questions is a different matter! Asking simple closed questions based on recall is easy; asking questions which develop thinking takes a little more thought. Using Bloom's taxonomy, questions which can be asked at key moments in the lesson can be planned for in advance of the lesson. This does not mean that you have to script everything that you will say, but that key questioning episodes can be prepared for with the text of the question ready. This will help you move away from simple recall questions to those which develop learning.

Another way in which Bloom's taxonomy can be used, either in its original form or the revision depending upon what your school requires, is in the preparation of incomplete stems which form the basis of questions addressing both lower-order and higher-order thinking. These incomplete stems can be prepared in advance, and many teachers keep a set of stems to hand for when the occasion demands. An example of such a list of stems, using both original and revision versions, is shown in Table 1.5.

Using these stems as a planning tool you will be able to develop questions in advance, but also be able to use them in the dynamic of the lesson taking place as it happens.

Table 1.5   Bloom-derived question stems

Knowledge/ *remembering*	Describe . . . Describe what you are doing . . . Show me what you are doing . . . Can you remember how to . . . Identify . . . Can you recall . . .
Comprehension/ *understanding*	What is the idea behind this . . . Can you show me an example where you . . . What differences are there . . . What is going on at this point . . . Can you demonstrate . . . Explain . . . Illustrate . . .
Application/ *applying*	How will you go about . . . What will you do to . . . Can you think of (*or show me*) an instance where . . . How will you carry out . . .
Analysis/ *analysing*	How might it have been different if . . . What happens in the bit when you . . . Can you explain what went on as you were doing that bit where . . . Compare that with . . . Can you distinguish between that and . . . Are you able to describe how you . . .
Synthesis	What would happen if you were to put your ideas together with hers . . . What would happen if you changed that bit where . . . How could you do this differently . . .
Evaluation/ *evaluating*	What was successful . . . What changes might you make . . . Can you justify . . . How do you feel about . . . Why do you think that . . . Are you able to suggest . . .
Creating	Can you come up with a solution . . . Are you able to devise . . . Can you generate . . . How about a different response . . . What would that look like . . . What would that sound like . . . How would that be made up . . . Can you produce . . .

Source: Fautley and Savage (2007: 37)

Conclusion

One of the key messages that runs throughout this book is that it is thinking about teaching and learning which is key to delivering successful lessons. Hopefully by talking through the various elements and components of a lesson, this has equipped you with the resources to be able to achieve this in the specific context of your school and your teaching within it.

Summary

In this chapter we have looked at the common components which go into planning for a lesson. We have thought about the three-part lesson and its derivatives. We have considered a range of common components of a lesson plan, including starters, plenaries, aims, objectives and episodes. We have thought about teaching styles and how they can best be used to effectively deliver teaching and learning. We have also considered what sort of things constitute a learning episode. Sequencing learning is of key importance, so we have spent some time thinking about how this can be planned for.

Knowledge is another important element of learning so we have considered types of knowledge and ways in which teachers can address higher-order learning with their pupils. This took us to the vital teacher skill of questioning, and we used pre-planned question stems for asking good questions in the classroom.

Reflective questions

- How can you involve a variety of lesson episode types within your teaching?
- What sorts of knowledge are you concerned with in your pedagogy? How can you best foster and develop these in your pupils?
- Have you broken down the topics you teach into a series of smaller steps? Are there difficult topics you have to teach where small steps would be very beneficial to the learners?
- What sorts of questions do you ask? Have you tried asking a colleague to categorize them for you?
- What makes for a good question in your context? Do you ask good questions?

2 Lesson planning itself

In this chapter we consider aspects of planning that entail thinking about the whole lesson, we discuss some of the common pitfalls that can be encountered, and we think about what lesson planning can, and importantly, cannot achieve. We have already discussed how, when observing experienced teachers in action, much of what goes on is invisible. It is probably this aspect of pedagogy that has led some, including those in governments of all hues, to believe that being a teacher is all about having good subject knowledge. It is our contention that this is only part of the equation and that good subject knowledge is not of itself alone a sufficient precondition to make a good teacher. In Chapter 7 of this book we discuss Shulman's (1986) notion of 'pedagogical content knowledge'; for the moment we want to think about what the role of teacher and learner are in planning for learning, and what can be achieved.

Depending on where you are on the continuum of novice–expert teacher experience, there will be some variation in the amount of time you find you *need* to spend planning for lessons. We know that at the outset teachers spend a huge amount of time in planning and preparation. If we think of this in ratios, the time can easily be 10:1, in other words a one-hour lesson requires 10 hours of planning. Clearly this is unsustainable in the long term, especially in a full-time teaching position. As teachers progress along the novice–expert continuum, we know that they get quicker at planning. But this happens incrementally, so the 10:1 ratio reduces to 5:1, and so on, down to 1:1. But this still means a lot of work. As teachers move towards expert status, we would expect the planning to take less time than the lesson takes to deliver. But there are exceptions to this too, for instance, when a new topic is being introduced for the first time, when a new class is being taught, or when a lesson is being observed perhaps.

In this book we want to make a clear distinction between two activities which although related, are in fact separate. These are:

- planning for learning;
- filling in a lesson plan template.

The first of these, planning for learning, entails thinking about what will be learned in the lesson, what activities will be undertaken, what learning episodes will be appropriate, what questions asked, what resources needed, and so on. The second of these, filling in a blank lesson plan template, involves making visible the first. Of course, it is logical to think about undertaking both activities at the same time, but this is not axiomatic. It is the thinking behind the lesson that takes most of the time. You may get ideas for lessons while you are teaching, when you think you could do something next lesson with this class, or even in a few weeks or months time. You will also get these ideas at odd times too, shopping, out with friends, on the bus, all sorts; some people say there is no such thing as an off-duty teacher! Capturing these ideas is important, but it is the mechanical documentation of filling in the form which can take a lot of teacher time. Throughout this book we are at pains to make one thing very clear, and we will keep repeating this point:

> *There is no magic lesson blank template which will solve all planning problems at a stroke. Such a thing does not, and never will, exist.*

This may seem an odd thing to say in a book on lesson planning, but we know from the many conversations we have had with teachers at all levels, from NQTs to SLTs, that many thousands of hours have been spent in schools in pursuit of this. So much so that we wonder if searching for the 'Holy Grail' of such a plan has actually taken teacher time away from planning for learning. This is not to say that a good lesson planning template is not needed, it is, and during the course of this book we shall be looking at this. But it is important to bear in mind that the template is not of itself the answer. We know Ofsted are concerned with teaching and learning as the result of planning, not the planning process in isolation from teaching and learning:

> Lesson planning is one of the issues most frequently cited by teachers as creating workload. Teachers often produce lengthy individual lesson plans, especially when schools are preparing for Ofsted inspections, as there is a common misconception that Ofsted inspectors require detailed written plans for every lesson. This can lead some teachers to spend a minimum of two hours a week just filling in lesson plan templates; time that could be better spent planning meaningful, motivating teaching.
>
> The Government wants to bust this myth by making it clear that neither the Department for Education nor Ofsted require written lesson plans for every lesson. Instead, inspectors may want to see where the lesson they observe fits in the sequence of teaching.
>
> The Government supports the idea that teachers should plan their lessons but this does not mean imposing a centralised planning

template on schools. A school's approach to lesson planning is a matter for the individual school, best achieved by the headteacher reaching an understanding with classroom teachers about what kind of planning is best suited to the school, its teachers and its pupils. There may be times when it is appropriate to ask individual teachers for more detailed evidence of how they plan lessons (for example if there is evidence of poor planning in the past). However, this should be the exception not the rule.

(DfE 2011)

This links closely to our description of the lesson planning process being distinct from lesson plan template completion.

What lesson planning cannot achieve

There is a myth among new and beginning teachers that the longer time spent planning a lesson, the more successful it will be. This attitude tends to manifest itself when classes are encountered which exhibit challenges to the teacher. We said at the beginning of this chapter that good subject knowledge alone is not sufficient for teaching, but we know that in schools where behaviour is not a challenge, and the possibility of expulsion a real threat, all sorts of things work which will not necessarily transfer to some of our inner-city or urban schools. In the cases where challenging classes are met, and we all have them, the issue of over-planning can become a real problem. We know of trainee teachers who have spent so long planning for these classes that when they come to teach they are already exhausted! This helps no one. Lesson planning is, as we have said, linked to behaviour management, but it is not the sole solution. Other factors need to be considered too, including whole-school approaches to behaviour for learning and the consistent application of rewards and sanctions processes which should already be in place. Lesson planning alone cannot guarantee good behaviour.

Another thing lesson planning by itself cannot do is to ensure that learning takes place. There is a common staffroom cry of frustration along the lines of 'I don't know why they haven't learned it yet, I've taught it to them hundreds of times!' The answer here is that because it has been taught does not mean it has been learned. Indeed a maxim for teaching everywhere can be expressed using a simple mathematical symbol:

$$Teaching \neq Learning$$

In other words, teaching does not equal learning. Reasons for this are manifold, but it is an important message. Its implications are enormous. You can plan the greatest all-singing, all-dancing lessons ever, but if in their execution little or no learning is taking place, then you have wasted your time. Planning needs to be done systematically, and in Chapter 1 we discussed breaking down learning into episodes. But it is important that even as these episodes are taking place the teacher is reflecting on what is going well and on what needs adjusting. Doing this is true assessment for learning, which we will deal with in Chapter 8. It also means that there is a serious purpose in asking teachers to reflect on their lessons and evaluate what has taken place with a specific focus on the learning. In the early stages of their careers teachers tend to focus on evaluating their own teaching, and it is only after some time has elapsed that they begin to think about learning.

This shift in focus from teaching to learning can be represented graphically, as shown in Figure 2.1. What Figure 2.1 means is that there is a balance to be achieved between a focus on teaching and a focus on learning. With experience, and over time, teachers move further to the right of this figure. This does not mean that reflecting on teaching becomes less important, but that more experienced teachers think about the balance between teaching and learning, and evaluate teaching by considering the effects that it has on learning.

From our perspective in thinking about lesson planning, it is appropriate to think of lesson planning as part of a cycle which begins with the evaluation of the previous lesson, this then informing what will take place in the next lesson. The reason for discussing reflecting on teaching and learning in the way the last few paragraphs have been is that it is important to consider the way that learning has been progressing. This will have a significant effect on the way you plan for the next lesson. It also prevents you planning a term's worth of lessons in one go. If you teach the same thing to parallel classes, you will know that 9Z can go racing ahead while 9X are still struggling to get to grips with the basic concepts. As we said, teaching≠learning! So evaluating

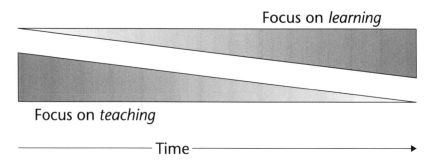

Figure 2.1 Shift from teaching to learning.
Source: Fautley and Savage (2008: 127).

learning at the end of a lesson helps you to know where to pitch the start of the next lesson. A useful technique is to do this as soon as possible after the lesson. We know that schools are complex, and that this means that teachers have to deal with a myriad of issues at the same time, so taking a few moments to do this at the end of each lesson will mean that it is still fresh in your memory.

What should a lesson plan include?

There are many views on what a lesson plan can include, and there are many variations on the lesson planning documentation that schools expect their teachers to fill in. This means that what you are required to do by your school, higher education institution (HEI) or teacher training programme may differ from what we discuss here. This does not mean that either view is wrong, simply that there are many variations on what is viewed as important.

Depending upon where you are on the novice–expert continuum some information about the class may be required. Even for very experienced teachers it is helpful to know who are the pupils with special needs, who are gifted and talented, and which pupils fall into other cohorts, for example, English as an additional language, looked after children, children from problematic home backgrounds, children of prisoners, children who live between a number of addresses, and many others. This information is of use in planning for differentiated and personalized learning within the lesson.

We have already discussed aims and objectives. The importance of these should not be overlooked. They are a significant feature of the lesson planning process, and help to place what is being done into a logical and sequential context. We have also looked at intended learning statements. Again, these are important in bringing the lesson to life, and in ensuring that what is being taught and learned is of direct relevance to the class. As we shall discuss in Chapter 8 on assessment, written well, a good intended learning statement becomes its own assessment criterion.

Which leads us to the body of the lesson, where we have suggested that you think about, and plan for, a variety of learning episodes to take place. In doing this there is always an imperative to think about how long each episode should take, and we have already emphasized the importance of timing and timekeeping. One way in which the lesson planning template can be of assistance with this is when learning episodes within a lesson are shown with timings. An example of this is given in Figure 2.2.

This shows the timings involved in a 75-minute lesson which starts at 10.00 a.m. The timings on the left of the figure show progression through the various episodes. In this example many of the episodes are in 10-minute blocks but there is no necessity for this to be the case. Planning a lesson in this way helps to visually break down the episodes so that you can see what order to do

Times

Figure 2.2 Outline lesson plan with timings.

things in as you move through the various stages. However, it is during the delivery of the lesson that you will find out whether the timings you planned for are realistic or not! It is important that the lesson plan is not treated as a fixed and immutable object from which you cannot ever deviate. Differences between the *planned lesson* and the *delivered lesson* should be evident in the way that you as teacher make professional judgements concerning the ways in which things take place. So deviating from the plan is not only acceptable, it is to be expected. This is another invisible aspect of more experienced teachers' pedagogy, and another point that we re-emphasize throughout this book.

When novice teachers deliver a planned lesson, they often tend to do so sequentially, with all of the activities being undertaken in order. Due to the often unforeseeable nature of classroom life, this can lead to situations where the final practical activity can be started with, say, only two minutes left to run! The way in which more experienced teachers avoid this problem is by shifting their attention away from sequentially operationalizing the lesson plan, and instead constantly monitoring the sequence of the lesson so as to decide what needs to be altered in order to arrive successfully and without stress at the endpoint. These two perspectives are represented visually in Figure 2.3.

What Figure 2.3 shows is that experienced teachers plan sequentially, but operationalize their within-lesson thinking, what Schön (1983) might refer to as 'reflection-in-action', from the end of the lesson backwards. In other words they know from the lesson plan what they want to cover, but they are simultaneously monitoring their own performance so that this can be accomplished within the span of the delivered lesson. If this means things need to be jettisoned in order to reach the end of the lesson, then so be it. The problem of over-running is especially acute when novice teachers' lessons run over the bell going for the end of the lesson. Good behaviour management does require an orderly end to the lesson, and so this needs to be planned for and enacted. Likewise if things are going more rapidly than planned for, then the teacher knows they can allow more time to be spent on some activities than they had originally envisaged. This contrasts with the sequential unalterable delivered lesson of the novice teacher. Knowing this may be of use in helping novice teachers with what mentors often say is a key problem for them, that of timekeeping.

This distinction between the *planned lesson* and the *delivered lesson* is a key one, and is another theme we return to during the course of this book. It is important to bear in mind at all times that the lesson plan is a guide, not an end in itself. It is the way the lesson plays out in practice that is important for the learners. They will not know how many hours have been put into honing the lesson, they will only be aware of what happens in the classroom. As the quotation from the DfE at the start of this chapter showed, it is apparent that what Ofsted will be concerned with is the quality of the learning experience.

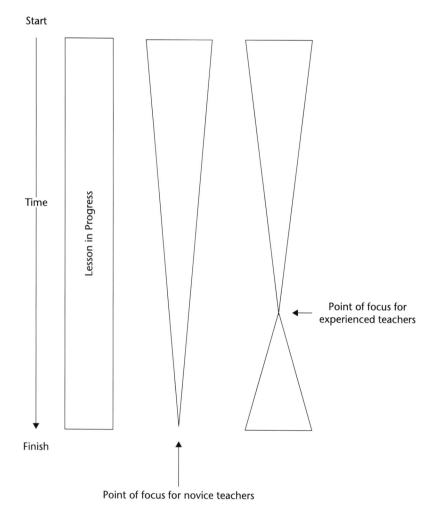

Figure 2.3 Novice and experienced teachers' foci of attention.

Common pitfalls in lesson planning

This discussion of timing takes us towards thinking about some of the other common pitfalls to be found in lesson planning. Timing figures significantly here, but other pitfalls relate to the appropriateness of material taught and availability of resources.

Apart from lesson over-run, another common planning pitfall is to over-allow or under-allow for some aspects of the lesson. After a while you will know that it takes, say, about five minutes to get the equipment ready for a certain sort of practical episode, so planning that this can be done in 90 seconds is unreasonable, likewise allowing 10 minutes for it is simply a waste of time. This does not mean that you need to become a sort of classroom time-and-motion monitor with a stopwatch, and harangue the pupils if they take 10 seconds too long in getting things ready!

In some ways linked to this is a tendency for beginning teachers to try to pack too much into the lesson. The lesson they have planned contains far too many activities, teaching episodes and practical work to be achievable in the given time. During the course of the delivered lesson these points become apparent, but because they still are operating in the way shown for novice teachers in Figure 2.3 they are not able to do anything about it. Sharing plans with mentors and more experienced teachers helps significantly, especially as this over-stuffing tends to occur at the start of a teacher's training.

As a corollary to this, having experienced over-stuffing, sometimes beginning teachers follow this with under-scheduling. Having had far too much in one lesson, they then react by planning only one thing for the subsequent lesson. Inevitably the pupils then finish this learning within a few minutes, leaving the novice teacher wondering what to do for the next hour.

Another related issue is over-specification of activity sequences in lesson plans. We have seen examples where things are planned for in unnecessary detail. If the pupils need one special measuring scale ruler per pair from the stock cupboard, then details of which order they will be given out can be too much (although there can always be a reason for things in the classroom, and as an observer, these are questions worth asking). Likewise listing every tiny detail of what is to be done can also be over-specifying. If the pupils need to work from page 56, that is fine, but writing into a lesson plan to say 'now 9Z, I want you turn to page 56 in your text books, that is the one with the heading in green followed by blue writing' is probably too much. This represents an over-emphasis on filling in the lesson plan template at the expense of thoughtful planning for learning.

Another frequently encountered pitfall, especially common among trainee teachers, is to plan a lesson for an idealized class, as opposed to the real one that will be receiving the lesson. This tends to involve a number of problematic features, including not recognizing the strengths and weaknesses of the real pupils in front of the teacher, not taking into account the nature of the learners as they really are, and, particularly alarming, not taking the prior learning of the class into account at all.

It is this last point which tends to cause the most problems for the teacher when they come to the delivered lesson. It seems obvious when pointed out, but the sequence of learning needs both planning *and* monitoring to ensure that what is planned for is learned, and that what is needed has been dealt with. Knowing the prior knowledge of a class is obviously easier with time, after all, if you are the teacher you will know what they have done previously. For teachers new to a class, this information may not be quite so immediately accessible, but nonetheless it does need to be looked into.

Another area often neglected by novice teachers is the issue of equipment availability. It is often the case that some costly items of equipment are available on a shared basis, and there is normally a way of booking or a rota system so that such articles are fairly distributed. Novice teachers sometimes assume that they can have equipment at any time, and so plan lessons accordingly. Clearly this will not work, and lesson planning needs to engage with school systems already in place, however informal they may seem.

Another pitfall is where the planned lesson, when put into practice, transpires to have some problematic aspects which require correction in delivery. For novice teachers, thinking on one's feet can be a skill which has yet to be acquired, and so correcting these flaws takes rather more time than would normally be expected. This can affect the flow of the lesson, and as with so many things in teaching, can also lead to behaviour management issues if unchecked.

This discussion of common pitfalls is not intended to be exhaustive, but it is meant to illustrate some of the issues and to point to more general planning issues which need to be taken into consideration when thinking about teaching and learning.

Who is the lesson plan for?

Lesson planning is in many ways a difficult activity to engage with. We know that it is one which teachers across the novice–expert continuum continue to find problematic. There are many reasons for this. Planning for learning is complex, and involves the teacher in an activity which only partly relates to the way the lesson will be delivered. Let us clarify what is entailed in that last statement. It is undeniably the case that professional expertise of teachers is an invisible part of their pedagogic practice. This is true whether it applies to teaching and learning, pedagogic content knowledge, behaviour management, crowd control, or sheer presence in the playgrounds, public spaces, corridors, and classrooms of the school. We have all known teachers who walk into a classroom and simply by being there the class falls silent. These attributes, always built up over time, are carried with the teacher as part of their invisible cloak of professionalism. It is doubtful whether these attributes are directly learnable. If they were, we could teach all novice teachers how to silence a class simply by walking in. We know it is not as simple as that. So within the activity of planning for lessons, teachers need to be aware that they bring with them their own personal baggage of teacher persona. This means that planning for learning, certainly by novice teachers, needs to be planning for themselves.

This is why the process of planning only *partly* relates to the way the lesson will be delivered. Indeed, the same lesson plan could be delivered in entirely different ways by two different teachers.

What this all means is that we need to give some attention to the issue of who the lesson plan is actually for. There are a number of possible audiences for this, including:

- the teacher
- the head of department
- the rest of the department
- a university tutor
- the subject mentor
- the professional mentor
- the learning coordinator
- the SLT
- governors
- Ofsted
- the pupils

Each of these will have different requirements and different reasons for wanting the lesson plan. But the primary audience should always be the first and last people on this list, namely the teacher and the pupils. It is unlikely that you would want the pupils to actually see the lesson plan (especially as it should contain information about personalizing learning for key named pupils), so they are the audience for its delivery, whereas the others on the list may well want to be involved in seeing the planning process in action, or reflect on its outworking in the lesson itself.

This means that different levels of detail may well be required, depending on who the audience is. For an experienced teacher planning an unobserved lesson for themselves to deliver it may well suffice to have a brief outline of what is required. For an observed lesson it is quite possible that more detail will be needed. Depending on why the lesson is being observed may well affect the level of detail that can reasonably be expected in the lesson planning document. This is a point which many novice teachers fail to grasp. They often complain that 'real' teachers do not spend many hours staying up half the night, as they do, planning lessons. This is because of the invisibility we spoke of before. Experienced teachers are able clearly to differentiate between the planning process and completing the lesson planning blank template. For novice teachers the two are inextricably bound together. So although experienced teachers often appear to have little by way of detailed lesson planning documentation, the reality is that the detail is there but invisibly located in their heads. Asking novice teachers to produce detailed lesson planning renders it visible, and, importantly, amenable to discussion, and suggestions for improvement can therefore be readily made and incorporated, a point we return to in Chapter 11.

But in all of this it is easy to lose track that the real purpose of a lesson plan is to facilitate learning; this should always be at the forefront of attention. While you may be able to impress lesson observers with your plate-spinning skills in keeping lots of disparate activities going on at the same time, if the people who observe your lesson know anything at all about education, they will want to see the effect that you are having upon the learners. In relation to this, an interesting question to ask yourself is this:

> In this lesson, who is working hardest, me, or the pupils?

There may well be good reasons why in some lessons we would want to see the teacher working harder than the pupils. However, many seasoned lesson observers say that when watching *learning*, as opposed to watching teaching, they expect the pupils to be working *at least* as hard as the teacher. Is this the case for the lessons you are planning and delivering? If an observer came into your class, what would they see more of – teaching or learning? This takes us back to the point we stated earlier on in this chapter, that teaching≠learning. You can be teaching away, but very little learning could be taking place. So, how do you do something about this? This is a point we will address particularly in Chapter 8 on assessment.

The starting point for lesson planning

We have looked at the various ways in which lesson planning needs to take into account a wide variety of factors when planning for learning, so let us turn our attention now to the beginnings of the planning process.

In later chapters we discuss how an individual lesson needs to be seen as one of a series, which have their origins in the planning evidenced in a unit of work. Throughout this book we ask a series of key questions which the teacher planning the lesson needs to consider. These will often be simple restatements of, or variations upon these three:

1   What do I want the class to learn?
2   Why do I want them to learn it *now*?
3   What do I need to do to enable them to learn it?

For an individual lesson plan the starting point will be questions 1 and 2 from this list. These might seem very obvious, but we have already seen that many teachers start instead with the question 'what do I want the class to *do*?'. This is a very different question: the key point of schooling is education, not

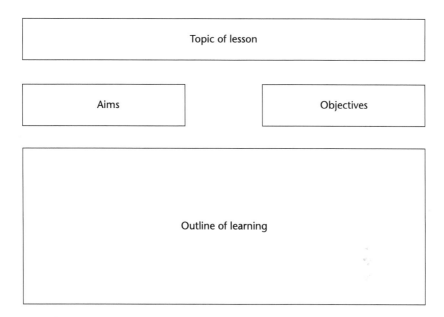

Figure 2.4 Initial lesson plan template.

child-minding, and so lessons should be predicated upon learning rather than activity. Knowing what you want the class to learn, it is then possible to move to the other questions in the series. Thinking about why this lesson should be delivered now, this should be apparent from the way in which the medium-term planning structure delineates delivery of the various elements of whatever the topic is. The next stage in this sequence is to ask what the teacher needs to do, and bear in mind the maxim we spoke of in Chapter 1 on common components, 'What is the minimum amount of information/instruction that the pupils need before they can have a go themselves?' To this end, some teachers find it helpful to begin with a fairly minimal planning template and use this to develop initial ideas. Such a template is shown in Figure 2.4. From this initial template further and more complex ideas can be added later. However, as we discussed above, it is the thinking that is the key element of the lesson planning; filling in the documentation is a distinct activity.

Summary

In this chapter we have discussed aspects of the lesson plan itself. We have differentiated between the thinking that goes into planning and the filling in of blank lesson planning templates. We have observed that teaching does not equal learning, and that it is learning which should be the key aspect of the lesson plan itself, as well as the enacted lesson which results from it. We have looked at the ways in which experienced teachers plan in the heat of the moment by having a point of attention which is not the end of the lesson, and have discussed how doing this is an important aspect of developing expertise in teaching. We have thought about episodes that can occur within a lesson and how these can be planned for. The important aspect of timing has been revisited, and we have pointed out some of the common pitfalls that can occur in lesson planning. Finally, and most importantly, we have discussed how it is learning that should be at the heart of all lesson planning, and thus it is learning, rather than teaching, which should lie at the heart of all good lessons.

Reflective questions

- Where does the main focus of your reflections lie, teaching or learning?
- How do you manage a lesson when you realize your planned timing is awry? Have you ever still been teaching when the bell goes?
- Have you encountered any of the pitfalls we discussed in this chapter yourself? How did you deal with them?
- How do you plan for changes between episodes? How do you operationalize these in practice?
- Have you started to think about sequencing learning?

3   Pedagogy and the plan: bringing it to life

Throughout this book we emphasize that lesson planning has a close and vital link to your emerging pedagogy. Your lesson planning will have consequences for your actions within the classroom. We have seen that it is important to make explicit and constructive links between the time you spend planning lessons and the time you spend actually teaching. To this, we would add a third and vitally important period of time: the time you spend reflecting on and evaluating your work as a teacher. This triangle of activity underpins the vast majority of your work as a teacher. Within this chapter, we are going to explore this triangle in some detail and think about how you can make those constructive links between these three key activities.

Lesson planning and curriculum development

Lesson planning, of the type we have been discussing in this book, can be a solitary, private activity. It involves many different skills, including diagnosing and setting appropriate learning objectives, choosing relevant and purposeful teaching activities, designing assessment and differentiation frameworks, assembling or producing helpful resources and much more besides. This private process comes to life within the classroom. You, the teacher, are the one who embodies the lesson plan and presents it to your pupils. Your pedagogy is the vehicle by which this embodiment and transformation can take place. For this reason, numerous educational thinkers, researchers and writers over the decades have emphasized the importance of the teacher in the process of curriculum development. This led Lawrence Stenhouse, a professor of education at the University of East Anglia, to famously state that there is 'no curriculum development without teacher development' (1975: 142).

Perhaps you find this a curious statement to make. After all, the processes of curriculum development, which include lesson planning of the type we have explored together in this book, can be done away from the classroom in a private space, and perhaps not even by teachers themselves (just have a look at the vast array of curriculum materials written by educational 'experts' you can buy online). But this line of thought misses the key point that Stenhouse was making. For him, and for us, there is an intricate and intrinsic link between the processes of planning that a teacher undertakes and the pedagogy that they adopt within the classroom to present the fruit of that planning process to their pupils. To explore this further, we will spend some time considering each of the main 'characters' in this scenario: first, you, the teacher; second, the pupils.

Teaching involves your whole being. Who you are is as vital as what you teach. As one teacher famously quipped, 'You don't teach your subject, you teach yourself!' While this assertion has a significant and important element of truth within it, most teachers are concerned with teaching a subject, or topic, and not about self-promotion! However, the statement does ring true in a more fundamental way. At all ages, in our experience, pupils do look up to their teachers (even though they may not always show it); they respect them and they are, for many, role models in various ways. Who you are as a teacher, how you behave, how you speak, how you administer praise or reprimands, how you deal with injustices, whether you are efficient and organized, and a whole host of other general attributes, are all noticed consciously or subconsciously by pupils. These things matter to pupils, and their parents, and they learn from them. Clearly, none of these things have anything to do with the subject you are teaching. They are about your professional role as a teacher.

As an aside to this opening paragraph about the importance of establishing an appropriate professional identity in the classroom, the most recent set of Professional Standards for Teachers emphasizes that teachers need to maintain an appropriate professional identity both inside *and outside* the classroom. This has significant consequences for the way in which you conduct yourself in public settings too.

So, in a general sense, in your teaching role you are embodying important general 'ways of being' that pupils will learn from. As we have seen, these will include models of behaviour, communication and collaboration (with pupils and other teachers), and your seriousness in promoting active engagement with the opportunities for teaching and learning in your classroom. But, second, in a more specific way, whether you are teaching in a primary or secondary school, you will be the vital first point of contact in relation to the specific subjects that you teach for your pupils. For secondary school teachers, the science curriculum may be in place but you, as a teacher of science, represent that subject – day in, day out – for your pupils. Like it or not, you 'live' science for them by the way that you act and behave in the classroom. This has significant consequences for the way you teach science. If you are bored by the curriculum that you are offering, can you really expect your pupils to be interested and engaged? The same is true for primary school teachers. While you will have to teach a broader range of subjects and topics than your secondary colleagues, the same key point is true for you too. You need to be a passionate advocate for all the subjects that you teach, whether or not you feel that you are a specialist in that particular area. In this sense, pupils really do take the lead from their teachers. If you want them to be enthusiastic about your subject, then you will need to be enthusiastic about it. If you want them to be engaged and motivated to learn in your subject, then you have to provide that earnest and serious approach to their learning that they deserve.

So, is there no curriculum development without teacher development? Stenhouse's key phrase shows us, as teachers, that if we are serious about our intention to develop the curriculum we offer to our pupils in this way, we cannot but help develop ourselves as teachers too. The two things go hand in hand. In terms of the planning process specifically, it will be important to remember that your own sense of teacher identity informs the process of planning. How do you feel about the lesson plan that you are putting together? Does it capture your imagination? Are you finding it hard to make natural links between various sections of the lesson? Is the narrative of the lesson clearly identifiable? If the answer to any of these questions is no, then it is probably unrealistic to expect the majority of your pupils to make sense of the lesson either.

More positively, build on your own sense of enthusiasm for a particular subject or topic in your planning. Look out for ideas and approaches that engage your imagination, act as triggers for your own curiosity and enhance your own intrinsic motivation. Design your teaching activities carefully in order to sustain that initial enthusiasm that pupils will have. Ensure that they have the correct balance of challenge while remaining within their capabilities. Choose your resources carefully. Make sure that they do not undermine the approach that you want to take within a particular lesson. Like you, they need to be 'on message' and chosen for a specific reason that enhances the lesson's central learning objectives. Think back to those lessons in your own education that excited you. Which ones stick in your mind? Why is that? Ultimately, remember that you are charged with teaching a particular subject, or set of subjects, but fundamentally who you are in the classroom is as important as what you teach.

An informed pedagogy: the site for teacher development

In the previous section, we urged you to consider the process of lesson planning as a significant element of curriculum development and as being fundamentally linked to your own development as a teacher. We emphasized that the time you spend planning your lessons in private needs to be cognisant of the fact that you, as a human being, are as important in your pupils' learning as the subject that you are teaching them about. How you 'are' in the class-room is as important as what you 'do'.

In this section of this chapter, we will talk about the development of an 'informed pedagogy' as the site for your development as a teacher. By 'informed pedagogy', we mean a pedagogy that is informed by your lesson planning processes in terms of who you are in the classroom, the subject content and the chosen pedagogical techniques that you are using within that lesson. In doing so, we will be getting down to some of the nitty-gritty of what you will be doing in the classroom, minute by minute, throughout your lesson.

Using learning objectives

As we have seen in previous chapters, establishing learning objectives for every lesson is a vital and integral part of every lesson plan. These learning objectives will have been designed to capture an essence of the learning for the lesson rather than merely describing the activities of the lesson (remember that they are a 'learning' objective not a 'doing' objective).

In recent years there has been a considerable debate about the role and function of learning objectives with an individual lesson. It is not unusual for us to visit schools where every lesson, regardless of subject, begins in the same way: pupils enter the room, they take out their planners and they write down the learning objectives for the lesson which have been displayed at the front of the classroom. When questioned, teachers report that this is an excellent way to settle a class quickly, it sets a focus for the lesson from the outset in the pupils' minds, and prevents the 'why are we doing this?' type questions that pupils often ask!

While this might sound quite reasonable, we do wonder whether this prac-tice negates any opportunities for learning as a journey or series of discoveries within lessons. Learning objectives might be communicated to pupils at other stages of the lesson, perhaps when a teaching activity has been completed and pupils really do feel like they have found something out for themselves for the first time. More fundamentally, you might want to consider whether pupils actually need to be told, week by week, what the learning objectives of the lesson are. Surely a good test of whether a lesson has been successful or not would be whether pupils can tell you what they have learnt without having to be told by you? This would be an interesting 'test' for any teacher to take. In one sense, whether or not what pupils say they learnt matches with what you think they should have learnt is immaterial. They might have learnt something much more interesting than you had planned! Clearly, in most cases we would hope that you would be able to use your chosen learning objectives in such a way as to stimulate learning in that particular area. But being too dogmatic about this could lead to problems. Being flexible in planning for what pupils learn, and the pace at which they learn it, is a sign of a teacher's competence and confidence.

So, consider carefully how you use the learning objectives in your lesson plan with your classes. Do not fall into the trap of a 'one size fits all' approach. Learning objectives should primarily be for your benefit, not the pupils. They will be written in language that may not be suitable for all pupils. You may want to write a more 'pupil-friendly' version for use within the classroom. The key point is that you have a strategy for their use that works in conjunction with the rest of your pedagogy within that lesson. In terms of using learning objectives within lessons, basic options include telling the pupils what the learning objectives are at the start of the lesson, using them to structure a process of reflection through a plenary at the end of the lesson, or making reference to them at specific points throughout the lesson to help signpost and consolidate key learning as it occurs. However you use your learning objectives, do so in a thoughtful way that you can justify to others.

Valuing every pupil: appropriate learning outcomes

Alongside your learning objectives, the learning outcomes for each lesson are an important part of your lesson planning. As we discussed in earlier chapters, these will need to be explicitly linked to your learning objectives and are an important component of your assessment strategy. Defined appropriately, they will give you a clear indication of whether or not pupils are learning what you intended as they engage in various activities.

Like every element of your lesson plan, learning outcomes need to be brought to life in your lesson. Part of this involves them being meaningful to every pupil in your class. While it would be clearly impractical to have detailed learning outcomes written by you for each specific pupil in each class that you teach, there are important pedagogical strategies such as differentiation and personalization that you can adopt to meaningfully translate your learning outcomes for the benefit of each pupil. In Chapter 5 we will examine both of these important strategies in more detail.

However, at this point it is important to raise a key issue that, perhaps, is one of the most significant in terms of the difference between your early experiences of teaching as part of an initial teacher education course and your work as a full-time member of staff within a school. In the former, you are parachuted into a school for a period of time and expected to take over a selection of classes for a short period. However you are introduced, the pupils know that you are there training to be a teacher. As a full-time member of staff, you are there for the long term, pupils respond to you differently and your own sense of identity within the school is considerably stronger. You will be teaching your classes for longer periods of time, perhaps several years, and you will get to know the pupils within those classes really well. This has a major impact on your ability to plan appropriate learning objectives and outcomes for those classes, perhaps even with specific pupils in your mind as you do so.

A cohesive approach to teaching activities

We have written at length in the earlier chapters of this book about the design of engaging teaching activities that give pupils the opportunity to explore key concepts and ideas, develop their understanding of these and, hopefully, boost their intrinsic motivation to want to find out more. While the design of these activities needs to be covered in detail within your lesson plan, your classroom pedagogy needs to present these appropriately and link them cohesively to other elements of the lesson (e.g. starter activities, plenaries or other assessment strategies).

This will require you to be organized. Your lesson plan will contain a list of physical and virtual resources for the lesson. These need to be to hand (whether available electronically on a computer or located within your classroom) and in an appropriate form for easy distribution to your pupils. While some subjects make use of more resources than others, the organization of pens, textbooks, musical instruments, digital cameras, data-logging devices, or whatever else pupils will need to use in your lesson does not happen automatically.

Beyond organization, teaching activities need to be framed appropriately both before the commencement of the activity, during it and afterwards. Pupils will need an indication from you as to why a specific teaching activity has been included in the lesson (this might be a chance to hint at a learning objective?) and how it relates to previous work they have done. Certain activities will need to be modelled by you (this is different from providing them with an explanation), and this modelling process needs to be practised carefully (remember, you can practise elements of your pedagogy like this without any pupils being physically present). During the teaching activity, pupils may need reassurances about their work, they may need to receive further support from yourself in some way, or be extended further if they are finding the basic activities too easy. Following the teaching activity, pupils will need a record of what they have done, what they learnt by doing it, and the implications of this for future work. Evidence of this may be produced in various ways depending on your subject area, but make sure that there is some trace of the activity left in the pupils' work. If the teaching activity has been well designed and successfully executed within the lesson, you will be wanting to refer back to it at key moments in future lessons.

An intelligent use of resources

The resources that you use to support your teaching are an important part of the way that learning is facilitated with your pupils. There is a considerable amount of research around concepts such as 'activity theory' that demonstrate how our human actions are informed and mediated by the tools or resources that we use (e.g. writing using a pencil and paper is very different from writing on a computer screen – beyond the obvious practical differences there are cognitive and psychological differences too). We will examine some of these ideas in more detail in the next chapter.

For now, your lesson plan will have identified the key resources that you require for your lesson. Your skilful use of these resources will aid the flow and pace of the lesson as well as provide a range of alternative opportunities to help your pupils engage with the learning objectives you have set. Be organized! Pupils really dislike disorganized teachers. Make sure all your resources are available and to hand. Check any pieces of technology that you are using prior to the lesson (and double check them!); make sure you have enough of them for use with your class.

More fundamentally, be reflective about the adoption of specific tools within the lesson. Even the best formed lesson plans may have miscalculated the use of a particular resource. Be prepared to be flexible and always plan for a way out of a particular activity if things are not going well. Many experienced teachers always have a 'Plan B' up their sleeve which is quick and easy to implement for when a lesson has gone off track!

Differentiation and personalization

Your chosen strategies for differentiation and personalization will have important consequences for the way you teach in your lesson. These will be explored further in Chapter 5, but for now it will be essential that you think through the consequences of these strategies for the use of your time in the lesson, as well as the time of other adults who may be supporting your work in that lesson. Alongside decisions about the allocation of your time in supporting individuals or groups of pupils, the pace of your lesson will also need to be considered. This a fine judgement; too fast a pace and you may leave some pupils straggling, too slow a pace and you may find some pupils getting bored and distracted. Getting the balance right here is difficult but there will be many ways that you can use differentiation strategies to help provide a personalized approach for each pupil in your class.

Assessment

Alongside strategies for differentiation and personalization, your lesson plan will have given some thought to an appropriate assessment strategy for your lesson. This is a central part of your pedagogy that will allow you to make judgements about whether or not pupils are learning what you expected them to learn within a particular lesson. In Chapter 8 we will be exploring this in considerable detail, including an analysis of the different forms of assessment and their implications for your pedagogy. For now, it is important to emphasize that your assessment strategy will work hand in hand with other elements of your lesson plan. It will be linked to your learning objectives and outcomes, have a part to play in the design and delivery of your teaching activities, and will also inform the strategies for differentiation that you have adopted.

Within the lesson itself, the best forms of assessment are seamlessly integrated within the various activities of the lesson. You can find out a massive amount about pupils' learning just by standing back and watching them working. Observation can be a valuable assessment strategy. The key thing to think about here is what you are going to do with the information drawn from those observations. Similarly, teacher-led or pupil-to-pupil discussion about an aspect of the lesson and the learning contained therein can be highly enlightening for you as a teacher. Again, having planned for an opportunity for such a discussion in your lesson plan and rehearsed and practised some specific questions to help stimulate the discussion, what are you going to do with the information that you have gleaned from the discussion? How will it be captured and help develop your future work with those pupils? Making judgements about the outcomes of pupils' work will also be a valuable assessment strategy. All teachers love marking, don't they? Again, marking work has an immediate benefit for the individual pupil (providing they look at what you have written) but there is also a major benefit for you too. You can quickly gain an overall impression of how that individual pupil is doing, as well as how that class as a whole has grasped a particular concept or activity that you have introduced it to.

Assessment, then, can have a vital role to play in helping you understand the impact your teaching is having on your pupils' development. This moves us into the final section of this chapter where we are going to turn our attention to the third key part of the triangle of activity that forms the bulk of your work.

Reflection and evaluation: two essential tools for continuing teacher development

In this final part of this chapter we are going to consider two vitally important strategies that constitute the third part of our triangle of teacher activity. The cognitive processes involved in reflection and evaluation help you make constructive links between the mental planning processes behind lesson planning and the intense activity of teaching itself. Used constructively, they will also help you improve as a teacher.

Right at the outset we want to emphasize that reflection and evaluation are not the same. Like differentiation and personalization, there are areas of overlap, but we will be considering each in turn in an attempt to disentangle some common misconceptions.

Reflection at the heart of your pedagogy

One thesaurus (Collins 2002) has the following entry for 'reflection': 'a calm, lengthy, intent consideration'; it follows this with words such as 'musing, rumination, thoughtfulness, contemplation, reflexion, meditation, introspection and speculation'. In the hurly-burly of school life, you might ask yourself whether reflection, while desirable, is possible! While many programmes of initial teacher education promote the idea of the 'reflective practitioner', how realistic is this for every teacher?

Before we answer that question, a more basic one needs to be asked: what does it mean to be a reflective teacher? Drawing on the work of Donald Schön (1983: 332–4), we think the reflective teacher does the following:

- They listen to their pupils and really seek to understand them as unique individuals, tailoring their instruction, speech and learning resources to respond to their specific requirements. Please note the links here to the strategies of differentiation and personalization.
- They think beyond their lesson plan in seeking to respond to individual students' needs and requirements. Again, this has resonances with your broader pedagogy. A well-constructed lesson plan can get you so far, but you need to be open and responsive within the classroom itself and, at times, willing to deviate from your lesson plan if necessary.
- They use the curriculum as an inventory of themes to be understood rather than a set of materials to be learnt. This is a contentious thought in the current educational climate. But, we would argue, it is an important one for you to consider. After all, is there not a difference between teaching a pupil something and educating them about it?
- They expand their knowledge of the pupils to encompass their learning and interests outside of the classroom.
- They use technology in a way to empower pupils to undertake their own learning rather than to reinforce old-fashioned, teacher-centric pedagogies. This has important links to the selection and use of appropriate resources that we will explore further in the next chapter.
- They prioritize independent, qualitative, narrative accounts of learning over blunt, accountability-driven assessment frameworks that depersonalize the pupils and their achievements. This will have important consequences for any assessment strategies that you might want to adopt. We will explore this further in later chapters.
- They challenge set theories of knowledge and its organization within the school systems of timetables and classrooms, seeking to make links in imaginative ways across and between subject boundaries.

While this list of attributes might seem daunting, reflective practice should start simply and quietly, in your own mind or in a private teaching journal. It should not be part of a grand-scale process of performance management or other accountability mechanisms. We think it too important to be compromised by them. You might argue that the general busyness of school life can compromise any well-meaning approach to develop a reflective practice. Clearly, this is a danger. But the writers on reflective practice recognize this and, more importantly, identify the larger structural forces at work in any organization that can compromise an individual's attempt to be reflective. So, how can you respond as a teacher? We suggest that you do the following:

1   Make a firm commitment to practise the art of being a reflective teacher.
2   Find a short period of time each day, even if it is just a few minutes, to reflect on the teaching you have engaged with during the day. Ask yourself simple questions such as:
    • What went well?
    • What did not go so well?
    • How could you improve things?
    • What would you do differently next time?
3   Keep a teaching journal, if not all the time at least for a set or specific period (e.g. the introduction of a new unit of work) to help you reflect more deeply on a specific intervention.
4   If possible, find a colleague to help share your reflections and act as a 'critical friend'.

Many of the broad ideas that relate to being a reflective teacher find resonances with the work of educational evaluation. In your early teaching experiences, you are most likely to come across evaluation related to the lessons that you have taught. In many courses of initial teacher education, students are required to evaluate each lesson. How can you do that in a constructive way that helps you develop as teacher? This is where our attention will now turn.

Evaluation at the heart of planning

> It is not enough that teachers' work should be studied; they need to study it themselves. (Stenhouse 1975: 143)

Education is a complex activity. It involves many different elements, including people, resources and ideas. As a teacher, watching education in action within a classroom or other learning environment is fascinating. Educational evaluation is a means of understanding the activities that go on within your classroom. It is a tool that you can use to investigate your own practice in a systematic and self-critical way. Evaluation involves many things and activities. It includes looking at things, asking questions, listening to others, describing events and making interpretations. It is a skilful activity that some writers relate to an art form.

We want to explore two key evaluation activities you can undertake that are complementary to the broader processes of lesson planning and your classroom pedagogy. Finding the links between planning, teaching and evaluation will help you manage your time effectively and avoid you being distracted from your key roles in the classroom. It will also make for a better process of evaluation and assist you in your own development as a teacher. The two activities are observing and communicating.

Observation in the classroom

As teachers, we are used to observing classrooms. It is a key aspect of our work. Effective teachers make time during their lessons to take that step backwards from the complexity of classroom interactions to observe what is going on. Using observation as a key component of your lesson evaluation strategy will enhance your wider pedagogy. However, familiarity with the classroom can be a barrier to effective observation. Therefore, it will be important to find ways to challenge your own observations. To this end, we will briefly consider a range of issues associated with observation that will help you do this.

First, learn to live with uncertainty in your observations. The notion of 'truth' within an evaluation is highly contestable. What you are watching is framed by notions of objectivity and subjectivity which you could spend a lifetime exploring. As a classroom teacher you do not have time to do that now! Rather, look for examples of activities which are 'credible and defensible rather than true' (Kushner 1992: 1). While you are observing, use your instincts as a teacher to look out for interesting responses that pupils make within the lesson, unusual responses within particular activities, or that spark of creativity that a pupil may show at a given moment. Accounting for these in a simple way through your observation notes will be important, even if it is a brief comment in your teaching journal that can be returned to at a later date.

Second, use a range of technology to help you with your observations. This could include audio or video recording. If you want to explore and analyse your own pedagogy, why not consider video recording yourself? After you have got over the initial embarrassment of watching yourself on film (or is that just us?), this can be a very enlightening activity. If you are able to use a laptop computer with an in-built web camera directed at the position where you are standing, then your pupils may not even know that you are video recording yourself. Recording yourself as a teacher is no different from those disciplines such as acting, dancing or athletics where video analysis is central to improving performance. Why should it be any different for teachers? The analysis of these materials can also reveal interesting points that you may miss in the busyness of a lesson. While this can be incredibly helpful and interesting, do not record too much. It takes a long time to review recorded materials, but the benefits can be significant if you have the time.

Finally, be focused in your observations. Your lesson plan has specific learning objectives and teaching activities. Try to focus on these in the early stages of your observation. But, as we discussed above, remember that these should not be thought of as being fixed in stone. They will develop as the lesson unfolds and you will need to be responsive to the outworking of these throughout the lesson that you have designed.

Communication in the classroom

Good communication is central to teaching and learning. Communication can take many forms and you will need to be alert for these throughout your evaluation. Non-verbal forms of communication such as gesture, body language or facial expression will all be important within your classroom, but verbal communication will probably be a major focus in all lesson evaluations. In particular, conversations between you and your pupils are an essential part of your work. As such, they present a vital opportunity for the evaluation of the lesson as well as for assessment purposes.

So, first, be natural in your conversations with pupils. Build on your existing relationship with the class, or the individual pupil, and seek to nurture conversations around your key learning objectives. But do this in a natural, not a forced, way. Second, take nothing for granted. Listen to the conversations that pupils are having between themselves during the various lesson activities. These often contain really important evidence that can usefully inform your evaluation. When watching pupils working, try to resist the urge to interrupt too soon. Maintain a critical stance and do not close down the possibilities for exploring alternative viewpoints when you do intervene.

Third, allow conversations to touch on elements of your teaching as well as focusing on pupils' learning. This can be difficult, and even awkward, for experienced teachers. But it can prove very enlightening. So, be bold! Take a deep breath and, perhaps, be prepared for one or two difficult conversations. The feedback you receive from pupils about your teaching can be extremely valuable. Fourth, do not depend so much on the pupils' voices and forget your own. Recent educational initiatives have given a priority to 'pupil voice' that many educationalists are now finding unhelpful. For some, the emphasis on pupil voice is nothing more than adults' 'copping out' and an 'abdication of their responsibilities' (Paton 2009). Perhaps a balanced view of teacher and curriculum development needs to reassert the role of the teacher as a professional. Within the sphere of lesson evaluation, your voice is as vital as anyone else's. So, do not underplay what you think and say about your own and your pupils' work.

Through these and other methods you will collect a range of evaluative data about your lesson. Remember that data can take many shapes and forms. One method that many teachers have found helpful is writing a teaching journal. This could contain short comments about teaching sessions, notes about your thoughts or feelings during the evaluation process, snapshots of conversations with pupils or other things that come to your mind and might be useful later on. From this data, you will need to construct your lesson evaluation. Your tutors may have given you a template; there are many others available online. Whatever format you use, there will be several key areas that you want to address.

Evaluate the learning objectives, outcomes and teaching activities

Most lesson plans have learning objectives, outcomes and teaching activities. These may well be drawn from your longer-term planning and relate closely to the units of work that underpin your curricula. It is a good idea to start your lesson evaluation by considering these elements. Look back on your learning objectives in light of the lesson you have taught. Were they met? If so, were they challenging enough? If not, were they too far removed from pupils' current level of understanding? In terms of the learning outcomes, did all pupils meet them? Who did? Who didn't? Why not? Did the teaching activities proceed as you had planned? Did some work better than others? How did the transition points between activities work out? Were they smooth and seamless? Were the resources that you chose appropriate for the activities? These, and other questions (see below), can help you chart the progress of your pupils' learning week by week.

Evaluate your own performance

As we have mentioned already, teaching is a skilful activity that, over time, you should improve in. However, this improvement does not occur by accident. It is the result of a deliberate process of practice and reflection. In each phase of your teaching, you will have key areas for improvement (perhaps identified at the start of your teaching placement) that you will want to reflect on. Your lesson evaluation is an ideal place to start this process.

So, use your lesson evaluations as a way to discuss the nitty-gritty of your teaching. Try to think in detail about specific elements of your pedagogy (e.g. how you questioned a pupil, how you modelled a specific process, how you used a new behaviour management strategy, where you stood in the room, your body language, your tone of voice – the list really is endless!) and discuss it briefly in your evaluation. And, most importantly, use this opportunity to set yourself another target in that area (for reflection on and evaluation later on).

Or, alternatively (or as well), perhaps your mentor has asked you to focus on a particular aspect of your pedagogy. They may have done this explicitly (i.e. you really must improve X or Y) or implicitly (i.e. you've sensed this might be an issue in their mind). Either way, the evaluations that you complete lesson by lesson are an ideal time to show a positive response to their advice and guidance. Done well, they can provoke constructive discussions in your mentor meetings and create a positive impression of your engagement and progress.

Evaluate your pupils' learning

Finally, it will be crucial to evaluate the learning that your pupils have engaged in during the lesson. Hopefully, part of this will be covered in your evaluation of the learning objectives, outcomes and teaching activities. But here it is helpful to be even more specific. You might want to highlight the progress made by one or two pupils specifically (i.e. name them and what they have managed to achieve). It would be certainly be appropriate here to talk about strategies of differentiation and personalization and how they have been applied to particular pupils (perhaps those with SEN or those who have particular gifts or talents).

Making judgements about a lesson

So, you have planned your lesson, taught it and reflected on it. You have observed pupils working and have talked to them about their work. In a parallel stream of activity, you have assessed their work in various ways, involving pupils in this process too. Your assessment data is collated and organized efficiently. You are faced with a collection of data drawn from your assessment and evaluative processes. It is time to make some judgements about your lesson.

One of the key ways of making judgements is to ask yourself questions about the data you have collected. This kind of internal questioning is essential to reflective practice. Your questions might include:

- What are the values that have underpinned this lesson? Are they from my experiences or beliefs, or are they from somewhere else?
- Who have been the winners and losers in this lesson?
- How have the processes of teaching and learning been connected in this lesson? How do I know?
- How would I describe my teaching approach in this lesson? Has it been authoritarian or democratic, formal or informal? What aspects of my pedagogy have changed or developed from a traditional, subject-based pedagogy?

- How have the pupils learnt in this project? In what ways have they learnt differently than they might have done in other lessons I have taught?
- Were my original learning objectives and teaching activities for the lesson appropriate? How did they change and develop over the duration of the lesson? Would I do the same lesson again?
- Whose knowledge really counted within the lesson? How did the knowledge base of my own subject specialism relate to the existing knowledge that pupils brought with them to the lesson?
- What would the consequences be of the changes I could make when I teach this lesson again (i.e. on myself and my pupils)?
- How does my evaluation of this lesson link to the broader processes of initial teacher education or continuing professional development that I am engaging in?

These questions may or may not be appropriate for you at any one given point in time. This is all part of a personal, analytical process. Learning to ask the right questions about the work you have undertaken is part of the process of reaching a judgement about the work. It is part of the process of becoming a skilful, reflective teacher.

Summary

This chapter has discussed ways that your original lesson planning can be brought to life within the classroom. By focusing on specific elements of your pedagogy, we have attempted to demonstrate how your lesson planning is an integral and vital part of becoming a skilful classroom teacher. Similarly, we have emphasized that what takes place once a lesson has been completed, by way of reflective and evaluative thinking, has an equally important part to play in your development as a teacher. It provides a vital channel of feedback into the planning process at the level of individual lessons, your broader process of curriculum development and your wider continuing professional development.

4   Resources for learning

This chapter is concerned with resources for learning, and the ways in which they figure in your planning for teaching and learning in the classroom. We are using the word 'resources' in as wide a sense as possible, and do not only mean physical resources, but also cognitive resources, thinking skills and the ways in which resources exist both as a means to a learning end, and as things to be learned about in their own right.

Activity theory

To begin with, we are going to use activity theory (AT) to analyse what is involved in planning. This might seem complex and difficult, but AT allows us to deconstruct the various ways in which the key elements, people and ideas involved are interlinked. What this means is that:

> Activity theory provides a unique lens for analyzing learning processes and outcomes. Rather than focusing on knowledge states, activity theory focuses on the activities in which people are engaged, the nature of the tools they use in those activities, the social and contextual relationships among the collaborators in those activities, the goals and intentions of those activities, and the objects or outcomes of those activities.
>
> (Jonassen *et al.* 1999: 159)

In this chapter it is the *tools* which are of concern, especially the ways in which they are used in learning. The construct 'tools' used in this fashion does not solely refer to physical artefacts, although they are clearly a good example; instead:

> Tools can be anything used in the transformation process (physical, like hammers or computers or mental, like models, theories or heuristics).

The use of culture-specific tools shapes the way people act and think. For the instructional designer, tools may consist of the design models and methods, the software production tools, project management system, or any other kind of tool that instructional designers use to transform the object (the instructional materials).

(Jonassen *et al.* 1999: 161)

Activity theory is concerned, as its name makes obvious, with *activity*, the components of which are organized in activity systems (Engeström 1999). 'In activity theory, activity is shaped first and foremost by an object held by the subject' (Nardi 1996: 39). The background to AT is that it arises from the research work of Russian psychologists Vygotsky, Luria and Leont'ev (Cole 1996). When discussing AT, it is usual to represent it diagrammatically by a series of interconnecting triangles, as in Figure 4.1. The key elements in the upper portion of this diagram are 'subject', 'tools', and 'object'. Tools form the basis of much of the discussion in the first part of this chapter. The terminology 'subject' in our case can be taken to refer to an individual, or a group of individuals, or a class of learners. The 'object' refers to that which arises from the activity using the tools. In other words the pupils, either collectively or individually, are concerned with producing an object, a learning outcome, which they do via the use of tools.

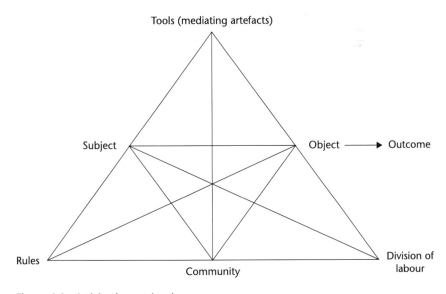

Figure 4.1 Activity theory triangle.

The base of the triangle concerns itself with aspects of the social nature of the activity, and we return to this later.

To give a specific example, Jennie Henley describes the activity of a group music session:

> In its most basic form, the subject is the student, the object is to play a piece of music and this is done through the use of tools such as instruments, musical notation, physical gestures etc. The individual cannot play the music without the instrument, and the instrument cannot play without the student, therefore it is the mediation between the two that fulfils the object of producing the music.
>
> But this is not an isolated process and a second layer has been added to place the activity within its social context and show where the outcome lies within the process of activity . . . an individual student will set themself a goal, for example to be able to play all the notes of a certain piece of music. The process they then go through to do this involves a complex set of interactions between their instrument and the notation, as well as the physical gestures that the conductor will give to inform the players where they are in the piece and how to play that part. This is within the context of where their own instrument fits with the other instruments in the ensemble, the rules that embody the nature of the ensemble, which in turn are guided by the context within which they are playing.
>
> (2008: 33)

This description can be applied to the majority of teaching and learning sessions delivered in schools, not only in music but in many other contexts too. Henley's account also takes us usefully into thinking about the nature of the tool itself. In her description, one of the tools is the musical instrument. This is obviously a complex thing; learning to play an instrument takes time, practice, skill and application. This means that many music lessons will be devoted to the primary purpose of learning to play the instrument. This is done both as a means to an end, and as an end in its own right. This is a very useful and highly transferable notion. All activity in lessons involving tools will necessitate some learning being devoted to using the tool itself before the tool can be put into use. We already have the example of the musical instrument but other tools can be much simpler, such as the pencil or the football, both of which, however, require a great deal of practice to use well. There are others of intermediate complexity, such as the pocket calculator and some that can be very complex, such as the computer. Others can involve significant health and safety issues, such as power tools in design and technology, or even the simple scalpel in science. Consequently tool use in pedagogy involves ensuring that safety issues are understood and observed. There is a wide range of tools used in schools nowadays, and you will know the scope and variety of this involved in the course of your annual planning for teaching and learning.

So, how does AT help? One of the principal ways is that it allows you to plan for teaching and learning of the various elements of the activity triangle as separate aspects within your pedagogy. This will involve progression from pedagogy about the tool, to using the tool, to developing proficiency of the tool, to using the tool in order to achieve something else. Let us look at an example:

Tool example: The magnetic compass

In essence, a magnetic compass is a very simple piece of equipment. Given no difficulties from electrical supplies, or other sources of interference, a compass needle will point to the north magnetic pole. There are many uses to which a compass can be put, including finding ways around the countryside using a map, orienteering challenges which involve doing this competitively and complex surveying applications and construction. The tool itself exists in a variety of types, from a simple circle with a needle, via the same with a rotating band for taking bearings, through to electronic devices such as Satellite Navigation devices with a digital display, and complex surveying technology.

Teaching and learning involving the magnetic compass will initially involve an understanding of the principle of the needle movement. This might involve a range of subject domains, including science, geography and design and technology. It can also involve art where pupils can design their own compass. From these beginnings the use of the tool will become more specialized, until the pupils are ready to put the application of the tool into practice. Although clearly obvious, it is unlikely that a group of pupils would be dropped off in Snowdonia in winter with a map and compass, and told to get to a specific grid reference for shelter and food! But at a more advanced stage, pupils may well be involved in similar way-finding activities, although we would hope that they began by finding their way around the high street using similar methods first!

In the example of way-finding in the tool example above, the AT triangle elements would be as follows: the compass is the tool, the subject is the pupil using it, and the object is to arrive at a given grid reference. The rules would be those of tool use, the compass points to magnetic north; the community would be the users of map and compass; and the division of labour within a group could involve some pupils taking bearings, others transferring them to the map, and maybe some acting as lookouts.

Although all of this is perfectly obvious in conceptualization, nonetheless new and beginning teachers often make rudimentary errors of sequencing learning materials by moving too rapidly towards using the tool in context, without the pupils gaining a clear understanding of how, why and when it should be used. If we consider the developmental pedagogic planning for this, we arrive at the situation shown in Figure 4.2. What this shows is that different lessons with regard to tool use will give rise to different learning objects, depending upon what is to be the focus of learning and activity. Hierarchical progression through tool use is shown by the descending arrows, the different objects arising from the lesson shown in the right-hand column. What is important in planning for teaching and learning concerning tool use here is

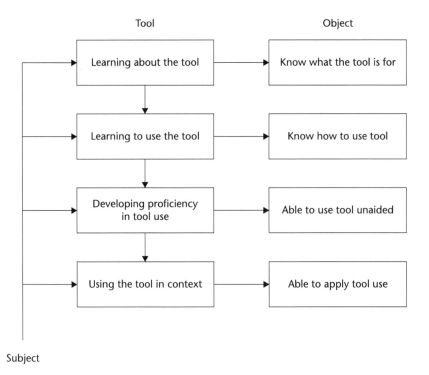

Figure 4.2   AT pedagogy of tool use.

that the teacher is clear in their own mind about the purpose of the lessons they are teaching concerning tools and their use. Of course, it is important to be able to put tools into practice as soon as possible, but teachers do need to spend time ensuring that pupils understand how to use the tool, as well as knowing what to do with it.

So far we have considered tools as being physical things, but they can also involve thinking skills and other concepts. For example, in mathematics, the notion of integration involves understanding the expression

$$\int_a^b f(x)dx$$

and being able to apply it when appropriate. The purpose of this mathematical expression is, to put it extremely simply, to find the area under a graph. However, some mathematics teachers have talked of having inherited pupils perfectly able to undertake the calculations required, but not having a clue what the tool of integration was for! This is a problem when teaching for understanding, and so use of the tool needs to preface, as Figure 4.2 shows, being able to put the tool to use in context.

Also important in AT is the notion of *rules*, and here it is appropriate to think about how learners are introduced to these. Clearly there will be a great deal of variation in rules of an activity involving tool use, and especially where health and safety are concerned, we would want these to be understood well in advance. Otherwise a commonly observed area of misunderstanding in beginning teachers is to try to work in too many rules too soon and to include in these the exceptions. It is here that Mrs Curwen's advice in her 1886 Piano method remains most appropriate, 'Leave out all exceptions and anomalies until the general rule is understood' (Curwen 1886, in Swanwick 1988: 133). This can give beginning teachers all sorts of problems and tie them up in knots! Yes, the exceptions are important, but they are probably best dealt with later, unless there is a pressing need to do so at the outset.

Division of labour is also a useful notion: it is not only a justification for groupwork (and vice versa), but it helps pupils think about ways in which they can cooperate on complex tasks, such as many real-world situations require. It also enables sharing the cognitive load in difficult tasks, parcelling out different aspects of this between groups of pupils, so that they can conjointly achieve something that alone they might not be able to (see ZPD in Chapter 7, pp. 100–1).

Having considered the planning processes involved in preparing for cognitive and physical tool use, we now turn our attention to a more detailed discussion concerning three different tools that are commonly found in classrooms and that may influence how you plan activities within your lessons. The three tools and their contexts are:

- teaching with interactive whiteboards;
- writing with word processing technologies; and
- researching with the Internet.

Teaching with interactive whiteboards

We can remember a time when teachers used a blackboard and chalk. In our own careers as schoolteachers, blackboards were gradually replaced by whiteboards and pens. In our visits to schools today, it is unusual to find a classroom without an interactive whiteboard. This march towards the almost wholesale adoption of interactive whiteboards presents an interesting context within which to explore how a particular tool impacts on your planning and teaching. In terms of activity theory, if the interactive whiteboard is the tool and you are the subject, the object will be the act of teaching itself. Clearly, this will have an impact on the bottom portion of the AT triangle (the rules, the community and the division of labour).

In the early days of interactive whiteboard use, we were constantly surprised by how un-interactively they were used! Positioned on a wall behind the teacher (who often worked in a 'presentational' style with a PowerPoint presentation displayed), early uses of interactive whiteboards were as glorified digital whiteboards. Pupils seldom got to interact with the board (apart from looking at it), and teachers resorted to the digital equivalent of 'chalk and talk' with their PowerPoint presentations (thereby demonstrating the old adage that those who rely on PowerPoint often lack power and seldom get to the point!).

More recently, interactive whiteboards have facilitated a greater degree of interaction between teachers, pupils and other learning resources. Partly this has been because teachers have had access to other technologies that have worked alongside the interactive whiteboard (e.g. digital slates, polling devices, iPad apps that link with the boards, etc.) but, more generally, teachers have just become more creative with their pedagogies and know when, and when not, to use the interactive whiteboard itself. It has become one of many potential tools that they can choose to use within their pedagogical repertoire in the classroom.

However, AT does provide an interesting lens through which to view the use of this tool and to ask constructive questions about how you might use it. For example:

- To what extent do I position the interactive whiteboard as part of my (i.e. the subject defined as the teacher's) usage and to what extent can

I utilize it to impact on the community within which it is situated (i.e. the pupils within my classroom)?

- If the objective for using the interactive whiteboard is to improve my pedagogy, how does this relate to the division of labour within the classroom? How can I ensure that the whiteboard is used in a truly interactive way to facilitate pupils' learning (and how does this relate to the facilitating role it might play in developing my pedagogy)?

There will also be some specific questions about the tool itself that you will want to consider. For example:

- What are the benefits or limitations of presenting information (whether text, image or video) with this tool? How does the interactive whiteboard itself impact on the sequencing of information, the retention of that information by pupils and the process of discovery (the 'learning journey') within a lesson?
- Is it possible to become over-reliant on the interactive whiteboard? What would happen to your teaching if it was taken away, or you had to teach in a room without this tool? Would anything change? (This is a good test to apply to any tool as you try to identify and analyse the precise impact it is having on your work.)

Writing with word processing technologies

This chapter is exploring how the tools that we choose to use within our teaching impact on our teaching as well as our pupils' understanding and learning. Having briefly considered the interactive whiteboard which, as we discussed, can unhelpfully become the preserve of the teacher in the classroom, let us turn our attention to a tool which is routinely used by teachers and pupils – the word processor.

Word processing technology – whether located within a particular piece of software, or in other locations with keypads or keyboards such as mobile devices – is pervasive in our lives. The ability to produce text on a screen as opposed to by hand is becoming the tool of choice for many pupils inside and outside of school. Does this matter? Is anything being lost in the process? The 'frame' of AT can help us analyse what is going on here. But before we do that, there is time for a little historical reflection. As this unfolds, see if you can spot some of the main AT concepts of tool, subject, object, rules, community and labour within this aside.

An historical aside

In a letter of 1916, T.S. Eliot reflected on how he felt the typewriter was changing his ability to write:

> When composing on the typewriter, I find that I am sloughing off all my long sentences which I used to dote upon. Short, staccato, like modern French prose. The typewriter makes for lucidity, but I am not sure that it encourages subtlety.
>
> (Eliot 1988: 17)

Thinking back even further, Carr (2010: 17–19) recounts the story of the famous philosopher Nietzsche who, suffering from many ailments that threatened to jeopardize his career as a writer, ordered a typewriter to be delivered to his lodgings in 1882. The Malling-Hansen Writing Ball was an object of great beauty that, with practice, allowed him to write up to 800 characters a minute. It was the fastest typewriter that had been made.

Nietzsche was so delighted with this technology that he composed a short ode to it:

> The writing ball is a thing like me: made of iron
> Yet easily twisted on journeys.
> Patience and tact are required in abundance,
> As well as fine fingers, to use us.

But, as Carr reports, the Writing Ball began to have a more subtle effect on Nietzsche's work. His friend, the writer and composer Heinrich Köselitz, began to notice changes in his writing style:

> Nietzsche's prose had become tighter, more telegraphic. There was new forcefulness to it, too, as though the machine's power – its 'iron' – was, through some mysterious metaphysical mechanism, being transferred into the words it pressed in the page.
>
> (Carr 2010: 18)

Köselitz's letter to Nietzsche is fascinating. In his own work, he said, his 'thoughts in music and language often depend on the quality of the pen and paper'. Nietzsche replied, 'You are right, our writing equipment takes part in the forming of our thoughts' (Nyíri 1994; Kittler 1999; Emden 2005; Cate 2005).

More recently, it was fascinating to read the famous American composer John Adams' reflections on how his musical composition process is still facilitated by paper and manuscript paper despite his having powerful digital composition and scoring software available (Adams 2013).

The stories of T.S. Eliot, Friedrich Nietzsche and John Adams demonstrate that the tools we choose to use for our writing impose limitations as well as open possibilities. 'We shape our tools', observed John Culkin, 'and thereafter they shape us' (Culkin 1967). Paraphrasing him, we could write that as teachers we choose our tools and thereafter they shape us and our pupils.

This short historical reflection provides a fascinating insight into the interplay that thinking with an AT mindset can provide. Within these stories there are specific subjects (writers and composers) working towards particular objectives (a poem, play or musical composition), working within particular sets of rules (stylistic conventions or grammatical frameworks), communities (of other writers, composers, publishers as well as readers and listeners) and potential divisions of labour too. Central to all these networks are the tools themselves (the pencil, pen, typewriter, paper, etc.).

Within your teaching, have you been able to stop and reflect on the specific differences that writing with a pen or pencil might have to writing within a digital environment? There will be benefits (psychologists would call these 'affordances'; Gibson 1979) as well as limitations. For example:

- Pupils may be helped, automatically, with their spelling and grammar as they use a digital tool. Is this automatically a good thing? When is it, and when isn't it?
- Pupils will think differently about ideas if they handwrite them. Researchers believe that handwriting is linked closely to cognition and this changes when digital tools are adopted. Are you aware of these changes and how they may impact on how pupils might engage with a specific learning task?
- The structure of one's writing changes as the tools change. Sentence construction varies, the ordering of paragraphs and the structuring of longer narrative structures may become more difficult as writing disappears off the screen. Does this matter? How can you help pupils to compensate for this? Are they using word processing tools skilfully to help combat any potential shortcomings within the writing environment? Do they know what these might be?

Researching with the Internet

The Internet is a powerful tool. It transforms many of the basic tasks that we do every day. From buying watches to scheduling meetings, updating personal profiles on Facebook and sharing key thoughts on Twitter, it is hard to imagine life without it.

There are many potential benefits from using the Internet as a learning tool. Research shows that many cognitive skills are substantially strengthened through its use. These include the strengthening of brain functions related to fast-paced problem-solving, recognizing patterns in a range of data and analysing their important characteristics, and making judgements about the quality of information contained within a particular source. One study of the way that British women searched for information on medical conditions revealed that the speed with which an individual was able to assess the value of a particular page of information increased as they gained familiarity with using the Internet. While an experienced Internet user was able to ascertain the value of a particular page in a few seconds, it took a novice user much longer to find out whether that information was trustworthy or not (Sillence *et al.* 2007).

Other studies have reported benefits in terms of small increases in our working memory. These increases allow us to become more skilful in juggling ideas, focusing our attention on competing ideas and analysing, almost instantaneously, their relative value. Small and Vorgan (2008: 21) report that for many of us this has led to our 'developing neural circuitry that is customized for rapid and incisive spurts of direction attention'. Using the Internet also improves a range of lower-level skills such as hand–eye coordination (through various gaming environments), reflex response and the processing of visual cues (Green and Bavelier 2003).

Developmental psychologists have explored the effects of different types of media on people's intelligence and learning abilities. The conclusion of Greenfield's recent work (Greenfield 2009) starts with the obvious thought that each medium, each technology, develops a particular aspect of cognitive skill at the expense of others. So, what does she have to say about the Internet? Her research indicates that the growing use of the Internet has led to a 'widespread and sophisticated development of visual-spatial skills'. But what is the trade-off? Greenfield suggests that the new strength in visual-spatial intelligence goes 'hand in hand with a weakening of our capacities for the kind of "deep processing" that underpins mindful knowledge acquisition, inductive analysis, critical thinking, imagination and reflection' (2009: 52).

Given findings such as these, writers like Nicholas Carr have argued that while

> the Net grants us instant access to a library of information unprecedented in its size and scope, and it makes it easy for us to sort through that library . . . what the Net diminishes is [Johnson's] primary kind of knowledge: the ability to know, in depth, a subject for ourselves, to construct within our own minds the rich and idiosyncratic set of connections that give rise to a singular intelligence.
>
> (Carr 2010: 143)

As teachers, what have you noticed about your pupils' use of the Internet? Has it diminished their ability to know, in depth, a subject for themselves? Is it a distraction or a source of interruption? Are your pupils aware of or taught strategies for collecting, curating and synthesizing knowledge and understandings from multiple sources?

As a tool, AT teaches us that the Internet is connected to a complex web of people, their community, their rules for engagement and operation, their division of labour and, perhaps most importantly in a teaching and learning environment, their objectives for learning. The Internet is an example of a 'mega-tool', something that encompasses so much by way of information, opportunities for sharing and communicating that it is difficult to reduce it down to manageable questions without resorting to trivial generalizations. But, for now, consider the following questions in light of our discussion about the tools we adopt within our classrooms and the consequences that these have for our pupils' learning and our teaching:

- What do you think are the benefits or limitations of using the Internet?
- What difference does using the Internet make on how your pupils learn about your subject?
- How does it make them think about a particular key concept within it, or link together ideas in different ways?
- What difference would it have made if you had given the information to the pupils in a different way, e.g. in a textbook or worksheet?
- What specific reasons can you give for choosing to use the Internet at a particular moment in a lesson rather than any alternative tool?

Developing our choice of tools in the classroom

This chapter has explored the framework of activity theory in relation to the tools we use within our teaching. We have argued that tools are not neutral in how they impact on the processes of teaching and learning. Tools exist in a complex web of interactions. The AT triangle helps us to broaden our understanding of how a particular tool exists within this web, allowing us to see how it has a range of affordances as well as limitations.

So, what should you be doing to help make informed choices in this area in respect of the tools you plan to use within your teaching? We would like to suggest a number of practical considerations for your work in this area.

1. Remember that the choices you make display the particular values that you hold

First, the choices of tools that you include within the classroom are a very real indicator of the values that you hold for your subject, as well as the particular pedagogy that you adopt to teach it. As we have seen with AT, tools are not value-neutral. They relate to you and your subject, as well as the objectives and outcomes for your use of them.

2. Weigh up the pros and cons of individual tools

Before adopting specific tools with your teaching, analyse the pros and cons. These will relate to the rules of engagement, the community within which the tool both is drawn from and used within, as well as the division of labour in terms of who is using the tool and for what purpose. We would urge you to consider the whole AT triangle (with all the various pathways and networks between its various nodes). There are always powerful, meaningful and beneficial uses of a broad range of tools that we can use in our teaching. But every tool has limitations too and the AT triangle can facilitate your exploration of these in a considered and thoughtful way.

3. Listen to a range of viewpoints

In considering your use of tools and technologies within the classroom, it is important to draw information and ideas from a range of disciplines. Within the world of education it is easy to listen to the latest educational guru or inspirational speaker. However, in forming judgements about the use of different tools within your teaching, it will be wise to listen to the voices of the sociologist, the psychologist and the technologist as well as the educator. While this may seem daunting, it is certainly worthwhile! Read broadly and develop an enquiring mind. We would advise you not to become a teacher who just follows the trend. Rather, seek broad counsel about the tools you consider adopting within your teaching.

4. Do not become over-reliant on one tool

As a general rule, do not become reliant on one particular tool within your teaching. If your pedagogy is, broadly speaking, a didactic one, you may find it comfortable and helpful to use a presentational technology like an interactive whiteboard. This is fine as far as it goes. However, the challenge for you will be to broaden your pedagogical approach where needed and to find tools to help support this development. If you teach the visual arts and you find that your pupils' work is becoming clichéd through the over-use of a particular piece of drawing software, this might be a signal for change. Uncritical use of the Internet as a research tool may be yielding poor results in a history project. Perhaps it is time to consider other sources of information retrieval. The examples could be endless and we are sure you will be able to apply this to your own work. You will need to pick the tool to do the job (so do not choose a chisel when a hammer is needed). However, if all you do is hammer all day, you will not produce a very good carving!

5. Do not allow technology to numb your senses

As we have discussed, all technologies impose limitations as well as open up possibilities. Part of the key here is choosing technologies that are appropriate to the tasks at hand and using them skilfully, with full knowledge of both the upsides and downsides. The AT framework we have presented in this chapter can really help you do this well.

Conclusion

In conclusion, the 'numbing' affect of technology has been well documented. Carr, drawing on Marshall McLuhan, writes:

> When we extend some part of ourselves artificially, we also distance ourselves from the amplified part and its natural functions. When the power loom was invented, weavers could manufacture far more cloth during the course of a workday than they'd been able to make by hand, but they sacrificed some of their manual dexterity, not to mention some of their 'feel' for the fabric. Their fingers, in McLuhan's terms, become numb.
>
> (Carr 2010: 210)

What is true for the fingers is true for the mind too. Carr goes onto illustrate this by reference to the work of the cartographer. The navigational skills of our ancestors were aided greatly by the invention of the map. It allowed them to travel across lands confidently, and had tremendous benefits in terms of trade and warfare. But this was at a cost. Carr continues:

> Their native ability to comprehend a landscape, to create a richly detailed mental map of their surroundings, weakened. The map's abstract, two-dimensional representation of space interposed itself between the map reader and his perception of the actual land. . . . The loss must have had a physical component. When people came to rely on maps rather than their own bearings, they would have experienced a diminishment of the area of their hippocampus devoted to spatial representation. The numbing would have occurred deep in their neurons.
>
> (Carr 2010: 211–12)

More recently, neuroscientists have noted a big effect on London taxi drivers' brains as they increasingly rely on GPS devices rather than the traditional process of acquiring 'the knowledge' (Dobson 2006).

Illustrations like these should warn us against being too positive or celebratory about the potential benefits of any one tool within our teaching. In our experience, while it is often easy to see the potential benefits of bringing a new piece of technology into a classroom, the downside of any piece of technology, in both physical and cognitive aspects, is often harder to identify and analyse.

As teachers, whether the choice of a tool comes from our own understanding, or whether it relates to a technology that is situated in the wider lives of young people, it is essential that our analysis of that tool and its use for educational purposes is carried out rigorously and conscientiously.

Summary

In this chapter we have considered how activity theory can be used to interrogate the way tools are used in the classroom. We have thought about how to teach for tool use, and how as teachers we need to begin by enabling pupils to learn how to use tools, whether cognitive or physical, before they start to employ them in problem-solving and real-life activities.

We have considered some specific and common examples of tool use in the classroom and problematized this. Finally we have suggested you give careful thought to the tools you choose to employ in the classroom, both in terms of their affordances, and in the effects they have upon thinking.

Reflective questions

- What tools do you need to teach pupils how to use in your lessons?
- Are you able to distinguish between cognitive tools and physical ones?
- Have you considered the sequencing of learning so that tool use is well understood before it needs to be used in earnest?
- How do you know your pupils are proficient in their use of tools?
- What teaching and learning tools do you have at your disposal in the classroom?

5 Differentiation and personalization: valuing your pupils

Your lesson plan contains a range of detailed information about your approach to teaching a specific class. In this chapter, we are going to consider how you can ensure that each individual pupil maximizes their learning opportunities within any individual lesson that you teach. To do this effectively, we first need to consider some of the broader issues concerning how pupils are organized within the school, in particular how they are grouped into the particular classes that you are teaching. This is normally done in one of three ways: streaming, setting or mixed ability classes.

Setting, streaming and mixed ability classes

Streaming and setting are both ways of grouping students by ability. Leaving aside notions of how 'ability' is defined (which is probably the topic for another book), setting is when pupils are grouped by ability within a specific subject, for example, a pupil could be in set 1 for geography and set 3 for maths. Streaming is when pupils stay in the same group for all subjects on the time-table, but they have been organized into class groups based upon some notion of their overall ability, for example, the results of their end of Key Stage 2 assessment for literacy. Mixed ability teaching means that pupils of all abilities within a school will be present in your class.

The grouping of pupils into streams, sets or mixed ability classes raises emotive issues in education. There is disagreement within public debates about which approach is the best for organizing pupils within the school. Those in favour of streaming or setting argue that children should be divided by ability so that all can be taught at an appropriate level; opponents of this believe that mixed ability teaching allows pupils to work unhindered by worries about their 'status'. In terms of educational research into this area, it is also the case that there is no consensus as to whether either of these two views are correct; as Ireson and Hallam observe: 'Although there is considerable disagreement in the literature, the weight of evidence indicates that selection and ability grouping do not have a powerful impact on the overall attainment of students' (Ireson and Hallam 2001: 17). However, this did not stop the then Government in 1997 publishing a White Paper, *Excellence in Schools*, which stated that 'unless a school can demonstrate that it is getting better than expected results through a different approach, we do make the presumption that setting should be the norm in secondary schools' (DfEE 1997: 197).

The arguments against setting and streaming focus on two areas, the academic and the social. As Richard Hatcher observes: 'The most overt mechanisms of social differentiation within the school system arise from processes of selection, both between schools, as a result of parental choice and school admissions procedures, and within schools, as a result of forms of grouping students' (1998: 494). This social argument says societal inequalities are mirrored in streaming and setting. This argument is amplified by Adam Gamoran (2002), who notes that 'minority and disadvantaged students tend to be over-represented in low-level classes'.

Arguments in favour of streaming and setting tend to relate to pupils being able to operate at their own speed, and for teachers to be able to address the needs of individual students. In one study, teachers told Smith and Sutherland that they found:

- It is easier to deal with a smaller range of ability.
- It was beneficial to separate those pupils with behavioural problems so that at least some could have a chance to learn.
- More able students could be challenged more easily.
- Mixed ability encouraged teaching to the middle and was inappropriate for a good number of students in the class.

(Smith and Sutherland 2003: 142)

However, the educational research literature explores a number of counterarguments to this viewpoint. Boaler's research argues that setting and streaming actually lower the results from those pupils in top sets, particularly girls:

Approximately one-third of the students taught in the highest ability groups were disadvantaged by their placement in these groups because of high expectations, fast-paced lessons and pressure to succeed. This particularly affected the most able girls.

(Boaler *et al.* 2000: 633)

Despite various advocates for and against setting, streaming and mixed ability teaching, and in light of the contradictory pieces of educational research, perhaps it is no surprise that there is still a mixture of approaches in evidence within schools across the United Kingdom. In 2010 a Freedom of Information request response was published by the Department for Education which stated that of the 18,400 classroom observations conducted by Ofsted inspectors in secondary schools in the previous year (2008/09), roughly four in ten represented set lessons (DfE 2012). The Government figures also showed that the majority of English, mathematics and science lessons in UK secondary schools are taught in classes which are set for ability. The figures for other subjects are harder to obtain, but many teachers of non-core subjects view their teaching as being essentially mixed ability anyway. As one secondary school art teacher observed, 'Although they come to art lessons in their modern language sets, they may as well be mixed ability for all the difference that makes.'

This comment reveals an important element in this debate which is directly relevant to the process of lesson planning – your expectations about a specific class. The educational research literature quite clearly shows that teachers respond differently when faced with the opportunity to teach a setted, streamed or mixed ability class:

> The great majority of teachers teaching sets expected a faster rate of work from the more able students (89%). In mixed ability classes there was less expectation that able students would work at a faster rate (69%). Whether students were in mixed ability or set classes, the majority of teachers expected greater depth of work from the more able students (86%). In mixed ability classes teachers expected more independent thought from the higher ability students (84%) than in set classes (76%). Most teachers expected the more able children to take greater responsibility for their own written work whether they were in mixed ability (71%) or sets (76%).
>
> (Ireson and Hallam 2001: 139)

The opening part of this chapter has presented a range of arguments for and against streaming, setting and mixed ability classes. Doubtless you will have opinions of your own, and your school may well have a policy which will affect how the classes you teach are organized. The key point for us is this: regardless of whether or not the pupils in the class you are teaching have been set, or streamed or not, anyone who is teaching more than one pupil at a time has a mixed ability class. To that end, the pedagogical processes of differentiation and personalization will apply equally to the lesson planning and teaching that you are doing for any class, however they are organized.

Differentiation and personalization: two sides of the same pedagogical coin

In the opening of this chapter we explored some of the ideas and educational research surrounding the organization of pupils into classes by ability (sets or streams) as well as more general mixed ability groups. Our key point is that to a greater or lesser extent, all classes are mixed ability classes because they contain individual pupils, all with their own set of issues and idiosyncrasies! The essential features of good teaching will remain the same, however the broader groupings are arranged. That said, it is important to be fully aware of the consequences of how particular groups of pupils that you are teaching have been formed. So, one of the first actions you should take is to find out about the prior attainment of all the pupils in your class. Having established this, you can then begin to plan constructively for them in your class. This planning process will involve you using two key, interrelated strategies: differentiation and personalization.

The terms differentiation and personalization have slightly different meanings in contemporary educational discourse. We will consider each term separately though, as you will see, there are many areas of overlap in theory and practice.

Differentiation

For us, differentiation is about a deliberate pedagogical strategy by which individual teachers create conditions whereby the curriculum is made accessible to individual pupils in ways which are appropriate to their needs, and which allow them to function to their fullest potential. In the early part of your teaching practice, it is helpful to think about planning for differentiation in two main ways – by task and by outcome. Although these are not the only ways that teachers can differentiate, they do cover the majority of the most common differentiation strategies that you will see teachers using.

Differentiation by task involves choosing different tasks within a lesson plan for different pupils or different groups of pupils. This can be a fairly major commitment, and may involve you having to do a considerable amount of extra planning. As Diana Burton observes:

> Differentiation by task requires a great deal of forward planning by teachers and a thorough knowledge of each learner's needs. While commercially produced material can be of some value, case-study research . . . has shown that teachers still need to devise their own differentiated support materials to meet each student's needs.
>
> (2003: 59)

Differentiation by task requires you to have planned carefully what the overall learning objectives will entail, and then have worked out pathways through this for groups of pupils within your class. One of the most common strategies that we have observed in recent years has been to divide the class into three main groups. The first group might be considered as 'average' attainers; the second group would be expected to make good progress and perhaps require tasks that are more challenging; the third group would need a greater degree of support and would find a simpler task more appropriate. Dividing your class in this way makes the process of differentiation by task a little more manageable. Clearly, the key point here is to make sure that the right pupils are in the right groups, and this would require a significant amount of knowledge on your part about each individual pupil and their educational abilities. In your early experiences of teaching, perhaps on teaching practice, this would require a detailed conversation with the teacher who normally teaches the class you are working with.

Differentiation by outcome occurs when students all undertake the same task, but produce different pieces of work from this. In some ways this is a much more manageable form of differentiation for you in terms of your initial planning. However, it is important to think really carefully about when this is an appropriate strategy to use. Some activities within certain subjects have a natural degree of differentiation built into them, for example, painting a self-portrait can be attempted by almost anyone but the outcome, in terms of the quality of the picture and the technical or artistic skills associated with it, will vary radically depending on who has painted it! Therein lies a major danger with differentiation by outcome. We need to acknowledge that there is a natural degree of differentiation by outcome in most teaching activities and natural learning environments. The point here is that differentiation by outcome should be chosen as a deliberate strategy. In other words, you need to consider, and perhaps define in a general way within your learning objectives, the learning outcomes of an activity in advance. This will allow you to move beyond the obvious and unhelpful stance of just accepting what pupils may do in response to a particular activity, and really use the teaching activity as a way to challenge pupils and move them forwards in their learning. Ideally, this needs to be reflected in your learning outcomes for the lesson. Like differentiation by task, you could imagine producing tiered statements of learning outcomes for a teaching activity that is differentiated by outcome. This would be a helpful framework within your assessment strategy for the lesson (of which more below). In the case of painting a self-portrait described above, clearly every pupil would produce an outcome of some sort. However, if your learning objectives focused on a particular aspect of shading and texture, then their outcomes could suddenly become more dramatic and differentiated as you would expect some pupils to demonstrate a firmer grasp of the artistic processes behind shading and texture than others.

Beyond differentiation by task and outcome, there are other forms of differentiation that you will find teachers using regularly. These include the following:

- **Differentiation by teaching resource** Different worksheets, materials, software packages or other forms of instructional materials are used at the same time in the class with different students or groups. In a way this a variation on differentiation by task, but with the notable difference that the students can be doing the same thing but by using different materials.
- **Differentiation by support** Learners receive different levels of aid from the teacher or from a teaching assistant. This can be an inclusion strategy and involves making the curriculum accessible to all the class. In the previous chapter we examined two ways in which you can do this by differentiating your time (and those of other adults supporting you in your classroom), and by the pace of the lesson.
- **Differentiation by questioning** We discuss elsewhere in this book the vital role that questioning plays in developing learning. As a differentiation strategy it can be used to focus specific learning possibilities on individuals or groups of students, by asking questions that lead to higher-order thinking or to different aspects of learning.

Carol Ann Tomlinson delineates the stages involved in effective differentiation by merging a number of these strategies:

> Effective differentiation is not random. Rather, it is based on a clear cycle of: (a) articulating what is essential in a topic or discipline, (b) assessing a student's standing relative to those essentials, (c) providing feedback and adapting instruction to ensure that each student progresses in the most effective ways possible to master the essentials, (d) assessing outcomes, and (e) making additional adaptations as needed.
>
> (2005: 264)

She also points out that differentiation is not about producing different lesson plans for each individual in the class:

> [W]hile it is true that differentiated instruction offers several avenues to learning, it does not assume a separate level for each learner. . . . Effective differentiated classrooms include purposeful student movement and some purposeful student talking.
>
> (Tomlinson 2001: 2)

Differentiation is a clear pedagogical strategy that every teacher will need to use. It needs to be described clearly in your lesson planning. However, what differentiation is not is an overbearing requirement to personalize everything to the nth degree, making your work impossible. Neither should it be a recipe for classroom disorder with individual pupils undertaking unrelated tasks or activities. What differentiation should be is a manageable approach to teaching and learning which uses materials, resources, plans or tasks to help pupils achieve their individual potential. This is a vitally important part of your pedagogy that is linked closely to the other side of this pedagogical coin – personalization.

Personalization

Personalization is the flip side of differentiation. Personalization, for us, is about ensuring that every individual child is given the best possible chance to succeed. Gilbert defined it as

> taking a highly structured and responsive approach to each child's and young person's learning, in order that all are able to progress, achieve and participate. It means strengthening the link between learning and teaching by engaging students – and their parents – as partners in learning.
>
> (DfES 2006: 6)

As teachers, you will encounter students with many different educational needs. Within any class you teach, your pupils' needs will be various and complex. Through strategies of differentiation, you will need to make adjustments to your own pedagogy in order to respond positively to them and give them the best chance to learn through your teaching. This will be a constant challenge to you throughout your career and it is one of the elements of teaching that can be most enjoyable. Nothing beats the thrill of seeing a pupil make progress as a result of a specific intervention that you have planned for and delivered through your teaching.

It will be no surprise to you by now that one of the most important elements by which you can do this will be through your lesson planning. This is not just about planning in terms of your subject or the knowledge that you want to try to impart. It is about planning the personalized processes of learning that the students are going to engage in during the lesson. This is an important distinction to get hold of. Although with any group of pupils of a similar age there will be a certain amount they have in common, planning the learning and the types of engagement that you are hoping pupils will have within the classroom involves you considering their ability levels, the structure of tasks (open or closed), the types of presentational approaches you might adopt (e.g. explanations or modelling), the progression routes within the learning, the particular tools you want to use (or get them to use), and much more besides. As you can see, providing a personalized approach to pupils' learning goes beyond adopting a particular differentiation strategy within a teaching activity. It is a way of thinking in the classroom.

Over the coming years there will be a increasing range of top-down, business-led initiatives which claim to personalize learning and result in more effective pupil engagement, cognitive acceleration, personalized visual, auditory and kinaesthetic learning styles, mental processing or whatever the latest educational catchphrase might be. We would urge you to maintain a critical approach to what seem like quick-fix solutions to something as complex as personalization within teaching and learning. While there may be valuable components within some of these types of initiatives, much of the psychology and neuroscience behind these innovations is at best only particularly understood by some of those advocating these approaches, and at worst deliberately manipulative. There may also be commercial agendas at play here which one should always be wary of. The motivation for financial profit behind many of these initiatives is very questionable and you should be very careful about adopting them within your teaching.

The pedagogical strategies of differentiation and personalization will, to a greater or lesser extent, implicate all your thinking about how to construct a coherent lesson plan and how to turn this into a meaningful set of learning opportunities within your classroom. In the final part of this chapter, we are going to turn our attention to two examples of how these strategies work themselves out with specific groups of pupils – those who have been identified as having special education needs and those who may be gifted or talented.

Teaching pupils with special educational needs

'Special educational needs' (SEN) describes the needs of a child who has a difficulty or disability that makes learning harder for them than it might be for other children of their age. It is a legal term that covers a broad spectrum of difficulties and disabilities. Many children will have special educational needs at some point in their education. As a teacher, it will be your responsibility to work as part of a team to support these children, adopting and implementing specific support to help them engage and learn within your classes. There are numerous 'types' or 'categories' of special educational needs. You can find a comprehensive list and description of many different SEN at http://www.specialeducationalneeds.co.uk/typesofsen-disability.htm.

Whatever form of SEN a student has, it is your school's responsibility to ensure:

1   the right of the child to have their SEN met through a broad, well-balanced and relevant education;
2   the right of the child and their parents to have their views listened to, taken into account and acted on if they are in their best interests;
3   the incorporation of children with SEN into mainstream schooling whenever and wherever possible, sometimes with the assistance of outside specialists working collaboratively with the school.

Once a child with SEN has been formally identified, a senior member of your school's staff will normally write an individual education plan (IEP) to help formulate a coherent approach to that pupil's educational entitlement in the school. This IEP would normally include:

1   what special or additional help is going to be given to that particular child;
2   who will provide that help and how often it will be delivered;
3   what help the parents can give their child at home to support the work being done by you and other teachers within the school;
4   the setting of some individual targets for that child's progress during the term or academic year;
5   a description of how and when the child's progress will be checked or assessed.

As a classroom teacher, you will have a vital role in supporting children with SEN. It is vital that you know which pupils in the classes you teach are on the SEN register. You will need to read their IEPs carefully and act upon the various individual targets within your lesson planning. This will require you to make individual provisions for certain pupils and adopt whatever differentiation strategy you feel is most appropriate in light of their individual targets. So, you may find yourself dealing with pupils with SEN who find it difficult to do some or all of the following:

- general work within your classes including reading, writing, number work or understanding information. For these pupils you might want to amend or adapt the resources that you are using to assist them in a specific way.
- expressing themselves or understanding what others are saying. This may result in you having to consider the social groupings in your class and the ways in which pupils engage with each other in different activities.
- making friends or relating to adults. Perhaps this is an aspect of support that extends beyond your individual classroom and will affect how these students are integrated into the life of the whole school,

but there is plenty that you can do within your own classroom to make these pupils feel valued and supported through your own teaching too.

Teaching gifted and talented pupils

Like your work with pupils with special educational needs, the provision of appropriate educational opportunities for pupils who are gifted or talented will span from whole school initiatives into your classroom. While the notion of a 'list' of pupils with particular gifts or talents has fallen by the wayside in many schools, there will be pupils in your classes who show an exceptional ability for your subject. It will be important to consider what individual provision needs to be made for these pupils. There are many ways in which you can do this. We will examine one such approach below.

Van Tassell-Baska (1998) provides a helpful framework for the analysis of your pedagogy in this area. Her curriculum theory for gifted and talented pupils identifies four key attributes that individual teachers need to consider:

- the level of the curriculum;
- the pace of the curriculum;
- the complexity of the curriculum;
- the depth of the curriculum.

The level of the curriculum relates to the way in which it will interest and challenge pupils. In some ways, it relates to the most basic differentiation strategies discussed above including differentiation by task and outcome. Her argument here is that the level of curriculum content, and how it is presented, must be at a suitable level for high achieving pupils. The pace at which the curriculum is offered to all pupils is important and an integral part of effective differentiation. It is something that all experienced teachers vary, almost minute by minute, in response to their analysis of how pupils are responding within a particular sequence of the lesson. Van Tassell-Baska argues that your gifted and talented pupils will be able to maintain a higher pace of learning than your average pupils. The key here is to find ways to facilitate a faster pace of learning for some, while acknowledging that others may require more time on a specific topic. Here, more sophisticated types of differentiation may be appropriate.

Van Tassell-Baska's third element relates to the complexity of the curriculum. This is not so much about the curriculum content (that, she argues, is part of the 'level of the curriculum') but rather it focuses on the capacity of gifted and talented pupils to engage in a number of advanced level ideas simultaneously. Challenging gifted and talented pupils at the level of ideas and advanced cognitive thinking is not new. However, it is important that you differentiate this from standard curriculum content and this will require a separate degree of lesson planning for these pupils. Finally, the depth of the curriculum relates to the opportunity of allowing gifted and talented pupils time to continue exploring an area of interest to higher levels, perhaps even reaching the level of an expert in a particular field of enquiry. Many gifted and talented pupils will show a considerable degree of intrinsic motivation and engagement when a topic or theme grabs their attention. They will want to run with this, explore it and mine it for new information. Allowing time for this when it occurs is difficult to plan for, but as with any element of lesson planning you should be alert to this and flexible in your pedagogy when it happens.

This brief discussion about the specific educational needs of pupils with special educational needs and those with particular gifts or talents highlights our overall point that all lesson planning needs to be done with a particular group of individual pupils in mind. All your teaching, whether with classes that have been set, streamed or anything else, are full of pupils with mixed abilities. Certain individuals may require more support for whatever reason, but how you use your time and energies within the classroom is, perhaps, the ultimate form of differentiation. You have to differentiate yourself! This is no easy task. You have limited time and energy and you will want to make sure that all pupils benefit from their time with you. Learning to use the strategies we have discussed in this chapter will take time but it does get easier with reflective practice, focused evaluation and experience.

Summary

In this chapter we have explored how processes of differentiation and person-alization can be adopted and used within your classroom pedagogy. Lesson planning underpins a learning journey. You start with a group of pupils in one location and, through your lesson, you travel with them to a new point. As with any journey, while it may follow a predictable route, there will elements of surprise and discovery along the way. Developing a skilful pedagogy is your main tool in facilitating both the journey and your pupils' individual responses to it. Part of this will involve you using the strategies of differentiation and personalization in tailored ways.

We have emphasized that every class is a mixed ability class full of indi-vidual pupils, each with their own educational needs. Thinking about plan-ning for an ideal or idealized class is pointless, so effective lesson planning has to take account of these real individuals. As pedagogical strategies, differentia-tion and personalization are not about producing an individual lesson plan for every pupil. They are about maximizing the opportunities for all pupils to learn through careful application of ideas, resources, support, time and energy. Pupils with special educational needs and those with gifts or talents will require additional thought and planning in conjunction with wider whole school policies and support frameworks.

For us, effective teaching and learning are centred on a strong relationship between you, the teacher, your emerging pedagogy and your pupils. All pupils deserve an education that is appropriately personalized to their educational needs. Every child matters and their education is too important to be left to chance. Focus on your role in the classroom, hone and craft your pedagogy and listen carefully to your pupils. These are the keys to an effective, personal approach to teaching and learning.

Reflective questions

- How are pupils organized when you teach them – sets, streams, etc.?
- Do you group pupils yourself within the class? If so, what criteria do you use for this?
- What strategies for differentiation does your school/department encourage? How are these manifested in your planning and teaching?
- Do you know who are the pupils with SEN and the gifted and talented pupils you teach? How do you personalize your planning for them?
- How do you ensure your planning for personalization actually 'comes alive' when you deliver the lesson?

PART 2

6 Metaphors for lesson planning and pedagogy

This chapter opens Part 2 of our book. Within this part, we are going to examine a number of broader educational themes and relate them to our book's central topic of lesson planning. In this chapter, we are going to broaden our understanding of lesson planning by using a number of metaphors and link this broader understanding to the development of your pedagogy.

Introduction

How would you describe the physical act of teaching? What does it contain? Clearly it involves you doing things – speaking, listening, moving, describing, explaining, assessing, analysing – and these things involve both your mind and body. But trying to pin down precisely what constitutes an effective pedagogy is tricky and it is not something that is easily observed. Skilful teachers are able to teach effortlessly, with an illusive quality that it is hard to describe accurately in words. As a beginning teacher, perhaps you are watching lessons delivered by more experienced teachers prior to doing some teaching yourself; maybe you are watching the exact lesson that you know you are going to have to teach in a few days time. But when the time comes to teach your lesson, despite your planning and preparation, the delivery of the lesson does not seem quite so smooth, the flow is a little more disjointed and, perhaps, the learning that the pupils engage with is not so intense.

The reasons for this are obvious. Planning and preparation for a lesson are important and build on skills that you can learn relatively quickly, but developing a skilful, practical pedagogy takes time. Experienced teachers are able to draw on years of practice. However, experience in and of itself does not equal an effective pedagogy. There are plenty of 'experienced' teachers whose pedagogy is often lacking and for whom teaching has become a mundane chore. As we saw in Chapter 3, the practice that teachers undertake has to be combined with a commitment to self-reflection and evaluation on a regular basis. Our advice for you, as a beginning teacher, is to place a firm emphasis on the development of your classroom pedagogy. Make the development of this skilful pedagogy your number one priority in the first few years of your teaching. But in order to do this, you need to settle in your mind a few foundational principles. What, exactly, is pedagogy and how does it develop?

The *Oxford English Dictionary* defines 'pedagogy' as 'the profession, science, or theory of teaching'. Other definitions of pedagogy extend this to cover the practice and process that underpin the activity of teaching. For example, Popkewitz develops a broad-based definition of pedagogy:

> Pedagogy is a practice of the social administration of the social individual. Since at least the 19th century pedagogical discourses about teaching, children, and learning in schools connected the scope and aspirations of public powers with the personal and subjective capabilities of individuals. This administration of the child embodies certain norms about their capabilities from which the child can become self-governing and self-reliant.
>
> (1998: 536)

Bernstein picks up on this notion of pedagogy as process, defining it as:

> A sustained process whereby somebody(s) acquires new forms or develops existing forms of conduct, knowledge, practice and criteria, from somebody(s) or something deemed to be an appropriate provider and evaluator. Appropriate either from the point of view of the acquirer or by some other body(s) or both.
>
> (1999: 259)

Note the ethical dimensions of a pedagogical approach in the above definition. The teacher, as an appropriate provider, acts in the role of evaluator (by valuing knowledge, skills and understanding) and developing appropriate forms of practice and conduct. This goes much further than just viewing pedagogy as the uncritical delivery of pre-packaged knowledge. This underpins our view that it is very difficult for you to teach successfully from someone else's lesson plan!

In recent years, one of the most influential figures in discussions concerning pedagogy has been Robin Alexander. A Fellow of Wolfson College at the University of Cambridge, and Director of the Cambridge Primary Review, Alexander defines pedagogy as: 'the act of teaching together with its attendant discourse. It is what one needs to know, and the skills one needs to command, in order to make and justify the many different kinds of decisions of which teaching is constituted' (2008: 11). Alexander makes the key, and hopefully by now familiar, point that pedagogy is not the same as teaching.

With resonances to Bernstein's quote, Alexander highlights the important justificatory elements of pedagogy that are all too often ignored within contemporary educational discourse.

So pedagogy involves teaching, but it is much more than that. It also involves an 'attendant discourse' that comprises the knowledge and skills which inform, justify and value the decision-making processes within teaching. Pedagogy is both a 'practice' and a 'process' through which certain things can be acquired or through which certain capabilities can be developed, justified and valued. In all definitions, references are made to something 'outside' the obvious context of an educational exchange (i.e. a teacher and pupil). In Popkewitz's definition, this is seen in the phrase 'scope and aspirations of public powers'; in Bernstein's by 'an appropriate provider or evaluator'; in Alexander's quote by his phrase 'attendant discourse'.

Skilful teachers embody a skilful pedagogy. They are responsible for its development and application. This skilful pedagogy does not appear by accident. It develops over a long period of time and needs constant nurturing through critical reflection, analysis and evaluation. Pedagogy is all the various elements of your thinking, planning and preparation that you do prior to a lesson, together with all the intellectual, physical and emotional aspects of delivering the lesson, as well as the processes of reflection and evaluation that you will undertake after the lesson has been delivered. In short, it is everything that you need to 'be' in order to be a teacher.

The focus of this book so far has been on the planning that you need to undertake. In Chapter 3, we considered how this planning relates to your work in the classroom. We encouraged you to consider the explicit links between lesson planning and how you bring that to life within the lesson itself through your pedagogy. We also emphasized that reflection and evaluation are key tools in making improvements to your teaching practice and providing feedback for your future lesson planning. But here, for a while, we want to ask some broader questions about how your lesson planning activities relate to the development of your broader pedagogy. In particular, we will focus on a number of metaphors that will help us think about how planning and pedagogy work together.

Teaching as science

The dictionary definition of pedagogy as the 'science of teaching' introduces our first metaphor: 'science'. Is it helpful to describe pedagogy as a science? We think this is a mixed blessing. There are many helpful aspects of this metaphor. Science, for us, implies a clear process of enquiry. It relies on key principles, appropriate methods, careful handling of materials, precision and rigour. Planning is a central component of 'doing' effective science. Like us, perhaps you remember practical science lessons where particular experiments were modelled by the teacher at the front of the classroom before being done by the pupils on benches around the laboratory. A key element of this approach is the experiment 'method', that has to be written up clearly and concisely as part of account of the experiment. It was not enough to merely find out the correct answer to a particular scientific problem. The process by which you have come to find out that answer has to be represented and accounted for in order for others to replicate that experiment and test your findings. Being able to write this process down in clear steps was an important part of 'doing' science well.

But there are limits to this metaphor. As we explored in the opening paragraph of this chapter, it is not possible to find the perfect mix of pedagogical ingredients and then mix them together in the desired quantities, according to a particular method, and – hey presto – effective teaching results! Teaching is built on human relationships and these do not lend themselves to be easily reducible to basic component parts. That said though, there is merit in the rigorous exploration of the specific elements or characteristics of a pedagogical approach. Finding ways of accounting for this in the 'method' of pedagogy would be a useful exercise for any beginning teacher. It would involve detailed and focused observation of a particular element of a teacher's pedagogy. For example, you might focus on a teacher's body language throughout part of a lesson: where do they stand/sit? (plot their movement); what posture do they adopt? (describe it in detail), and how does this flow from one posture to another?; how do they use their hands to emphasize key points? (when does this happen and how does it relate to the language they are using and the tone of their voice?); what, if any, barriers are there which inhibit their body language, and can these be removed? Or, to provide another example, you might focus on the technique of explaining a new concept: how is the explanation structured (does it have one)?; what hooks are used to engage the pupils' curiosity? (and are these are an *aide-mémoire* for pupils later on?); how are key points repeated or re-emphasized throughout the explanation?; what scaffolding devices are used?; are references made to existing knowledge structures and, if so, how are these extended?; what, if any, links are there to modelling and how does this differ from explanation? This kind of detailed, almost forensic, analysis of a specific pedagogical technique or device can produce very rich learning experiences for young teachers. However, as we emphasized above, just conducting the observation and finding out the 'correct' answer to your enquiry will not automatically translate into your being able to adopt an appropriate body language in the classroom, or explain new concepts better. Defining pedagogy as the 'science of teaching' has its limitations.

So, alongside this idea of pedagogy as the 'science of teaching', we would like to bring other metaphors into this debate. These, we trust, will help you think through the relationships between the physical act of teaching and the planning and preparation that you need to do in order to do this effectively.

Our next metaphor relates teaching to a type of 'performance'. In order to explore this in a helpful way, we are going to consider the work of three different types of performers: actors, musicians and footballers. Like teaching, all of these types of 'performance' and 'performers' require specific sets of skills and techniques, various pieces of knowledge and a broad understanding of the art form or sport they are working within. Like teaching, they also all require planning and preparation, often done in private, prior to a performance. We will start with the world of the theatre and the work of actors.

Teaching as acting

The theatre is a fantastic place that allows actors and audiences to dream together, be taken to new places and to enjoy and be challenged by new experiences. One of the aspirations of any theatre production is that the audience will leave the theatre changed in some way as a result of experiencing that production. This has many similarities to the processes of teaching and learning in the classroom. As teachers, we would all hope that our pupils do not leave our classrooms in the same state that they entered them! Learning should have occurred and this, over time, will result in cognitive and physical development.

With the exception of the most improvisatory forms of theatre (of which more below), most actors work with a script. In the majority of cases this script is fixed. It contains the words and other directions needed to perform the play according to the desire of the author. In many theatre traditions, for example, the Shakespearian, it would not be considered appropriate to change the words of the play, though, of course, many other aspects – such as the context within which the play is set, the staging of the play, the lighting and sound design – could all be developed in ways far from those imagined by the original play-wright. However, it is worth pausing and considering whether or not the script, which the actors have to remember and deliver using all their skills, is really 'the play'. As we have already hinted, the words of the script are framed by all kinds of other devices and structures. These would include the larger aspects of artistic direction such as a broader context for the play, the set and sound design, but they would also include elements that are intrinsic to the skills, techniques and work of an individual actor within this framework: the sound of their voice, the pace of their delivery, the emotional input they impose on the language, the way that they interact with other actors, and much more besides. Beyond all of these considerations are the audience, who constitute another layer of interaction with which the actor needs to communicate. How they respond to the events that unfold before them has an intrinsic effect on what any individual actor may do. They may 'play to the house' during one performance in a way that they would not do on another occasion. More broadly, certain elements, for example, set design, are likely to be fixed and unchangeable despite what an audience might think about them.

To what extent is this like the process of planning for teaching? At a basic level, the lesson plan document could be compared to the script. It contains the key sequences and instructions needed to deliver a lesson. The teacher plays the role of the actor and the classroom becomes the set, the context for the performance that plays a fundamental role in bringing it to life (or not). Finally, of course, the pupils are the audience, invited into this space for a particular performance and engaged and changed, we hope, as a result.

But the metaphor begins to fall apart because it places the teacher in the dual role of author and actor. Initially, the lesson plan has to be imagined and created. It is written by the teacher (author) with a specific group of pupils in mind, for a specific place (their classroom) at a particular time (Monday morning, period 2). As we have seen, all of these aspects (pupils, place and time) need to be considered carefully and the plan needs to reflect that level of specific thinking. It will present a set of ideas through a narrative that has structure (some kind of scene setting leading to the main events of the play), key ideas (characters or topics) and some kind of resolution within a set time period. But, second, the teacher is also the actor charged with bringing the script to life within a specific performance event (the lesson). Here, like the actor, they have to bring all their human qualities and attributes to bear in order for the performance to be engaging and convincing.

Teaching as musicianship

The second type of performance that we are going to reflect on here is that of musical performance, and the work of the musician. Like the actor, a musician is often required to work with a script (called the 'score') that has been produced by a composer. Many of the considerations that we gave to the work of the actor equally apply to the musician. The score is the basis for a performance, however, it does not contain everything that is needed in order to give a convincing performance. Like the actor's script, the musician's score has to be interpreted in light of a number of factors. These factors are informed by the musician's understanding of particular performance conventions that surround the period of time when the music was written or the style that it exhibits. So, for example, a musical score from the Baroque period of music (e.g. the work of J.S. Bach) would need to be approached in a different way to a score produced by a Romantic composer such as Rachmaninov. Part of this is because of the amount of detail that such a score may or may not contain. There is a general movement in the history of music for scores to contain more and more detail within them. For example, J.S. Bach might have been quite happy to tell his musicians to play quietly or loudly; Rachmaninov would have expected to communicate very precise instructions about the volume of specific passages of music within his score, as well as the gradual changes of volume that might occur over a period of time. The same is true of many other aspects of music's composition and performance. By the twentieth century, the score had become a very detailed representation of the composer's wishes that the performing musician had to take notice of and reproduce faithfully. By the end of the twentieth century, many composers had sought to replace the musician them-selves and communicate with their audience directly through tape, and later, digital recordings of their music which, to a larger extent, were under their own control.

This element of control with a musical score is only part of the story though, because all composers expect their performers to play within a particular style that is suitable for their music. Bach would have expected his musicians to provide embellishments to his score (perhaps by adding particular musical effects at key moments); Rachmaninov would have frowned on his musicians playing his music in this way. In many operatic styles, the practice of the Da Capo aria became the vehicle by which singers were able to show off their vocal virtuosity. Here, the basic structure of the aria (song) contained two main sections – part one and part two. Following part two, the first part would be repeated but it would be quite wrong for the singer to perform it in the same way as earlier in the aria. The singer was expected to take the basic ideas of the song (the melody) and transform it through their virtuosity into some significantly different. As opera shifted from a private to a public form of enter-tainment in the early nineteenth century, audiences would pay vast sums of money to hear specific singers (virtuosi) interpret these Da Capo arias in this way. This resulted in many composers, and others, complaining that the overall narrative of the opera was being hijacked by the singer for their own personal fame and notoriety.

There are some interesting comparisons here to the work of teachers in planning and delivering lessons. First, as with the previous example, teachers are in that dual position of creating the lesson plan (the score) and delivering it. Our exploration of the role of the score in musical performance raises questions about the amount of detail that may or may not be necessary in the lesson plan and the extent to which any individual teacher needs to be held accountable to the lesson plan as an integral part of their performance. As a beginning teacher, you may decide to include a lot of information in your early lesson plans but, over time, you may be able to provide the general structure within the plan itself and allow space for embellishment. The stylistic differences between different types of music have some relevance here too. As we will go on to see later in the book, the differences in subject approaches to lesson planning need to be borne in mind. These reflect more than just technical differences, but go right to the heart of what individual subjects really are and what they try to achieve as part of a pupil's formal education. Lesson planning should not look or feel the same for every subject. There is an important lesson here for those responsible for managing the curricula in our schools.

There is also an interesting element of audience (pupil) expectation here. To what extent should the lesson plan and the activities therein build on the 'legitimate' sense of pupil expectation within lessons? Like the Da Capo aria, the endless repeating of familiar ideas needs to be avoided so the skilful embellishments and improvisation that a teacher can bring to existing subject content are something that can provide endless challenge for the most experienced of teachers. No two performances of a Da Capo aria should be the same; similarly, no two lessons taught to any group of pupils will ever be same (even if they have the same or very similar lesson plans underpinning them).

Teaching as coaching

The third part of our metaphorical application of 'performance' within teaching brings us onto footballers. While you might characterize footballers as sportsmen or women, for the sake of our discussion here let's call them performers! We have chosen to focus on their work for a number of reasons. First, there are a number of similarities with the work of actors and musicians – they work in a group, they are highly skilful as individuals, and they provide a 'performance' (of varying quality perhaps). But in contrast to the vast majority of actors and musicians, footballers do not have a script or a score to work towards. Or do they?

The recent change in the manager of the England football team caused a lot of press speculation. While there was an initial momentum in favour of Harry Redknapp, the appointment of Roy Hodgson in May 2012 came as a surprise to many pundits. One of the concerns that was raised at the time related to the coaching style of Hodgson (Zonal Marking 2012). While a club manager, some professional footballers had found his coaching style too heavy-handed and laborious, involving them walking through particular team movements in what was seen as a stifling way. This was contrasted with the work of other football managers who, it was claimed, allowed their players a platform to exhibit their own flair and creativity. Harry Redknapp, some claimed, was 'all about individuals', whereas Hodgson was 'the ultimate system manager' (Zonal Marking 2012).

These approaches to coaching and team management can be seen by any keen football supporter. Sitting towards the back of a football ground, it is possible to observe the 'shape' of the football team ebbing and flowing as they move between defensive and attacking positions. The eleven players, while each being individually skilful and tactically aware, are playing as part of a larger team that has to be flexible enough to accommodate and rebut the advances of the other team while maximizing their own potential to attack and score when the right moment arises.

This curious reflection on the style of coaching that footballers receive gets to the heart of the relationship between lesson planning and lesson delivery. Taken to an extreme, the 'certain anarchy' (Zonal Marking 2012) style of management represented by the work of Redknapp could result in a pedagogical style that is all about a teacher's individual flair, exhibitionism and personal charisma. To these teachers, perhaps, the requirement for careful, systematic planning for learning that covers all eventualities (akin to the system management approach of Hodgson) is an anathema. But for others, a planning approach that covers every square inch of the field, and every eventuality, is seen as preferable. Within that clear structure, these coaches would argue, the individual flair of specific players can be nurtured and developed. For teachers following this model, very detailed planning might be seen as a requirement for teaching that will facilitate every pupil learning to their full potential.

But unlike actors and musicians, the footballer metaphor has one unique element – another team to compete against! The opposition are coached and drilled to exploit your own team and your individual players' weaknesses, and are there to beat you within the rules of the game. Here, we are not imagining the pupils as the opposing team! Rather, we would like to suggest that they do provide the challenge to any teacher's planning and pedagogy. The challenge is to match their planning and individual characteristics and flair to the development of a pedagogy that captures and inspires their imagination, making them enthusiastic about their learning and keen to participate fully in your classes. They will also provide that 'grit' against which your teaching will be honed. Often, very well behaved, passive classes are the hardest to teach well. A lively group of pupils who respond to your lesson (in good or bad ways) will often give you that immediate feedback that you need as a young teacher to change tack, provide additional support or more challenge.

Using metaphors to inform your planning

These three performance metaphors raise a number of key points for us to consider in light of developing links between planning and pedagogy. First, all performance activities do require preparation and planning of some sort. In acting, music and football, being well prepared with technical skills, stylistic awareness, communication skills and a good sense of teamwork are all necessary criteria for success. These things do not happen by accident. They require dedication over many years, regular practice, analysis and a constant focus on reflection and evaluation of one's own practice. While actors and musicians often work with a script or score, and this imposes certain restrictions on them, even footballers are working within a particular 'system' that may constrain the opportunities for any one player's individual action. In all cases, having a framework for artistic or sporting action is essential to the success of the activity.

Second, in all these metaphors there is a tension between the script, the score or the coaching strategy which all seek to impose, and the work of the creative actor, musician or football who wants to bring their own sense of personality and vision to the play, the piece or the game. You could characterize this through a sense of conformity or liberation. Perhaps the moments that an audience most value are when an actor, musician or footballer is able to take that step out of conformity and bring something that is unique and of the moment to that particular audience? However, that process of liberation can be taken too far. We would not want our Shakespearian actors to deviate from the script into some kind of free-form narrative; nor would we expect a right-back with defensive duties to abandon his team mates and adopt a careless forward role within a football game. For novice teachers, sticking with your lesson plan is a vital first step towards creating this link between planning and pedagogy. You have to lay the groundwork for a more liberated approach to teaching in the conformity of the lesson plan. There is no short cut.

Third, even with the most highly improvisatory forms of theatre, music and team management, there are mental frameworks and schemata within which performers work. This is important. Musical improvisation, when musicians apparently make music up on the spot (combining composition and performance together in the moment) is, essentially, an illusion. Improvisatory musicians have a framework of musical ideas in their minds, generated through hours of practice and pre-rehearsal; improvising jazz musicians have highly developed stylistic languages to draw on, developed through their listening to recordings, so playing one type of chord for Ella Fitzgerald might be highly appropriate while for Billie Holliday it would transgress her style. For teachers, making up lessons on the spot should be avoided, but experienced teachers will often talk about their best lessons coming to them in an instant, perhaps while doing something else completely different. These moments do not appear out of nothing. There will have been a systematic exploration of that particular field of subject teaching and pedagogy that underpins that creative moment. Creativity in lesson planning can happen, but it happens against the backdrop of hard work and effort (in our experience, 99 per cent perspiration and 1 per cent inspiration).

Planning, pedagogy and practice

Jo Salter was the first female jet pilot in Britain. Her account of learning to fly is fascinating reading and illustrates the variety of teaching and learning methods required to become a top pilot. Of particular interest was her account of how you can learn to fly without actually being airborne:

I used to walk around, rehearsing the checks, the switch positions, the radio calls – running circuits in my bedroom, plotting air defence tactics across a field, circling dogfights on bikes, even flying formation in my sleep. Rehearsal builds muscles in the brain and the brain remembers this much more effectively when flying and operating an aircraft. It is the beginning of an automated sequence where pilots react without thinking – essential for rapid decision-making at life-threatening moments.

(Salter 2005: 30)

When Salter began to train as a teacher, she began to relate this process of learning to the challenges associated with teaching:

As a teacher I employ the same lessons that I learnt as a student; I rehearse and visualise – how I am going to stand and how I am going to use my body language in order to convey my message. The spoken word is only part of how we teach. We have all experienced the flat teacher, the one who seems to no longer be there, whose energy has disappeared and whose presence is blurred. These are not the lessons you remember.

(Salter 2005: 30)

Much of this chapter has been devoted to forging an explicit link between planning and pedagogy. To these two Ps, we now add a third – practice. Practice is essential in turning your carefully prepared lesson planning into an exciting and stimulating series of opportunities for learning. But practice need not only be done in front of children. You can practise being a teacher all on your own! Salter's pre-rehearsal strategies and visualization exercises find common ground in the work of actors, musicians, artists and many sports people too. There are numerous ways that you can turn your lesson plan into a living enactment of your lesson and pre-lesson rehearsals are a vital part of turning a lesson plan into a reality. So, why not try the following?:

- Read through, act out or practise certain key parts of a lesson plan in private.
- Structure explanatory dialogue or key questions and, if necessary, mentally script parts of the lesson plan, ensuring that there is clarity and purpose in your words. These can be rehearsed in front of the mirror.
- Imagine responses to various different scenarios and planning courses of action. These need not be extreme situations. It may be something as simple as a pupil asking an awkward or seemingly irrelevant question. Having a number of good diversions or re-focusing

statements up your sleeve can smooth over potentially problematic exchanges.

- Rehearse a few jokes! There is a significant amount of literature that emphasizes the importance of humour in creating positive learning and teaching environments (Hill 1998; Garner 2005). While we may not all be natural wits, there is plenty of time to rehearse and practise a few, relevant jokes to insert with your lesson plan. Pupils will really enjoy this element if it is done well.

Summary: teaching, artistry and identity

In his classic book on pedagogy (Alexander 2008), Robin Alexander describes Douglas Brown, an inspirational and exceptional teacher at the Perse School in Cambridge during the 1950s. Perhaps not surprisingly, the teaching of Brown that Alexander describes throughout his chapter is very different from that which many teachers provide today. For example, Alexander reflects on the way that Brown talked to his classes (Alexander 2008: 156) as something that today would be considered a monologue. But Alexander explores Brown's intellectual, moral and pedagogical approaches which resulted, he says, in a display of the 'humility of genius and the artistry of teaching' at their best. The broad pedagogical approach Brown adopted led Alexander to describe him as not one teacher but four (language, literature, music and the man through the whom the power of these was unlocked).

It is notable that Alexander chooses to describe him as 'not one teacher but four', rather than 'not one teacher but three'. Brown's sense of personality and identity informed his teaching in powerful ways. The greatest subject that Brown taught was life itself. Within his English classes, individual subjects were subsumed through a skilful educational dialogue between teacher and pupil that we would be wise to try and recapture in our schools today.

Within this chapter we have explored the links between lesson planning and pedagogy through the adoption of various metaphors (teaching as science and teaching as performance). We have considered the work of other performers in significant detail and drawn inferences from their work to help our understanding of the links between lesson planning and the classroom where our planning comes to life. In doing so, it is easy to forget that your human character and personality are as important to the act of teaching as are the specific skills of lesson planning, explaining a concept or assessing a learning outcome. The early definitions of pedagogy quoted at the beginning of this chapter all hinted at that broader aspect of pedagogy as, in Alexander's words, an 'attendant discourse'. Never forget the example of Douglas Brown. It is the person you are that will provide the power to unlock a love of learning in your pupils that will span their lifetime.

Reflective questions

- What metaphors are the most appropriate for the ways in which you approach teaching and learning?
- Have you considered your role as a performer in the classroom?
- Do you change your role when teaching? If so, why is this?
- Have you observed an experienced teacher who makes pedagogy seem effortless? What lessons can you take from them?

7   Learning

We have said throughout this book that the most important focus of lesson planning has to be learning. In this chapter we discuss the topic of learning itself in some detail, consider theoretical approaches to learning, and think about ways in which you can apply these to your planning and teaching.

What is learning?

Whenever the topic of learning is encountered, discussion fairly quickly moves to the notion of *knowledge*. Indeed, many would argue that learning is all about gaining knowledge. A problem with this standpoint is that it treats all knowledge as being the same, and that this knowledge is therefore amenable to simply being given to people. We have already mentioned how novice teachers tend to hold views similar to this, and we also know that:

> Prospective teachers tend to believe that knowledge is a property that is created outside people's heads, and learning occurs when people absorb knowledge. The right thing for educators to do, then, is to transmit as much knowledge as possible to students and see that they memorise it.
>
> (Torff and Sternberg 2001: 20)

This view, of teaching as telling, is often referred to as the 'simple transmission view' of learning. This view can also be frequently encountered in other areas too, including the popular press, and, sadly (and potentially dangerously) among those politicians who over-simplify pedagogy solely as transmission from teacher to pupil.

More generally, simplistic views of teaching and learning are referred to by the American educator Jerome Bruner as 'folk pedagogies', and he counsels teachers to be aware of other people, including the pupils, holding these:

[I]n theorizing about the practice of education in the classroom (or any other setting, for that matter), you had better take into account the folk theories that those engaged in teaching and learning already have. For any innovations that you, as a 'proper' pedagogical theorist, may wish to introduce will have to compete with, replace, or otherwise modify the folk theories that already guide both teachers and pupils. For example, if you as a pedagogical theorist are convinced that the best learning occurs when the teacher helps lead the pupil to discover generalizations on her own, you are likely to run into an established cultural belief that a teacher is an authority who is supposed to tell the child what the general case is, while the child should be occupying herself with memorizing the particulars. And if you study how most classrooms are conducted, you will often find that most of the teacher's questions to pupils are about particulars that can be answered in a few words or even by 'yes' or 'no.' So your introduction of an innovation in teaching will necessarily involve changing the folk psychological and folk pedagogical theories of teachers – and, to a surprising extent, of pupils as well.

(Bruner 1996: 46)

This notion of folk pedagogies is a useful one to bear in mind both when thinking about your own views on teaching and learning, and, as Bruner observes, when talking about these issues with others. The reason that the notion of folk pedagogies has such a powerful hold on people is that the idea of something being simple and straightforward is appealing. After all, as H.L. Mencken may have, possibly apocryphally, observed, 'For every complex problem there is an answer that is clear, simple, and wrong.'

In order to consider why folk pedagogies and the simple transmission model are not sufficient, let us refer back to some issues which have been raised earlier in this book.

Types of knowledge

In Chapter 2 we started to discuss knowledge and observed that there are many ways of categorizing knowledge into different types. Let us look into this in more detail now.

One common distinction made is that between *knowing how* and *knowing that* (Ryle 1949). Here knowledge is divided between facts and processes. Indeed, this distinction is commonly encountered, with a variety of terminologies being employed to cover what are, in essence, very similar things. These distinctions and their labels include those seen in Table 7.1.

Table 7.1 Knowledge

Factual knowledge:	Procedural knowledge:
Declarative knowledge	Procedural knowledge
Knowing that	Knowing how

Declarative knowledge, Ryle's 'knowing that', is knowledge which can be declared, in other words, spoken. For instance, we can say that we know that London is the capital of England, that pork comes from pigs, that the Beatles sang, and that Aston Villa won the FA cup in 1887. *Procedural knowledge*, which Ryle described as 'knowing how', is knowledge concerning how to do something. For example, you may know how to play the piano, how to drive a car, how to play table-tennis, or how to bake a cake. These are all types of knowledge which require you to be able to *do* something, to perform an activity of some sort. This is an important distinction. You could be told, in a declarative fashion, the procedures which are involved when you are intending to ride a bike. This would probably involve something like this: 'Sit on the saddle, steer with handlebars, keep moving the pedals with your feet, and try not to fall off.' All of which seems to be very straightforward when uttered in a single sentence, but as anyone who has ever ridden a bike knows, it requires much more than this sentence of declarative knowledge in order to ride a bike! What will be needed in this situation is procedural knowledge. This also applies in many others areas of endeavour too; from the examples above we want people who can actually play the piano, play table-tennis, or bake cakes. Knowing how to do something involves more than being told by someone how to do it, it requires practising so that it can be done. We know that a person is able to do these things because they evidence their achievement in performance; someone who can play the piano does not demonstrate their mastery by describing what they do, they will sit at the keyboard and play some music.

In addition to Table 7.1 we also looked at cognitive and meta-cognitive knowledge earlier, which leaves us now a fifth knowledge type we want to explore in the context of learning. This is *knowledge of values*, what Swanwick and Taylor refer to as 'Knowing what's what . . . what we like . . . what we value' (1982: 7). Knowledge of values has a pedagogy associated with it, namely 'values education'. In Australia, the Department of Education, Science and Training (DEST) observed that values education

> refers to any explicit and/or implicit school-based activity to promote student understanding and knowledge of values, and to inculcate the skills and dispositions of students so they can enact

particular values as individuals and as members of the wider community.

(DEST 2003: 2)

This is a complex area, but one which affects planning for learning in many ways. For example, in assessment, which we look at in more detail in the next chapter, one of the questions often asked is: Do the pupils know what a good piece of work is? This involves making a *value judgement*, and in order to do this pupils need to understand what a good piece of work looks like, sounds like, feels like, tastes like, or whatever is involved, and, importantly, why this should be the case. Education for the development of values can be seen therefore to be of a different type and nature to education concerning declarative knowledge. In Chapter 1 we saw that in the original version of Bloom's taxonomy (Bloom 1956), evaluation was placed at the very pinnacle of the hierarchy of higher-order thinking skills. As evaluation clearly involves making judgements, then this sort of learning will need careful planning to avoid an over-simplistic 'mine is better than yours' slanging match. Teachers do need to do this, and do need to explain why one piece of work is better than another. But explaining to a class why a National Curriculum level 6 is different from a level 5 is of an entirely different order to trying to explain why Shakespeare is viewed by society at large as being better than *EastEnders*!

Having ascertained that learning involves some form of knowing, we can now turn our attention to theoretical descriptions concerning ways in which those processes of knowing can be accounted for.

Theoretical perspectives on learning

There are many separate theoretical accounts of learning. Despite this, or maybe because of it, it is not unreasonable to say that there is no one single theoretical perspective which we can use to account for all learning. What we do have is a series of viewpoints, positions and stances on learning which between them can be used to account for its various aspects. The reasons that we are discussing these here are that in order to plan effectively for learning you, the teacher, need to have some understanding of the ways in which pupils learn and how to maximize this by addressing their learning needs using suitable teaching strategies. You will also have some theories of your own as to how pupils learn. In order to take the learning of your pupils forward and develop it, you really need to give some consideration to *how* they learn, and it is learning theory that helps us with this,

From the many theoretical accounts, we shall for the sake of this book follow current conventions used in this area, and place theories of learning into three broad families. These are *behaviourist accounts*, *cognitive* or *constructivist* accounts and *socio-cultural* or *situated* accounts.

Behaviourist accounts

Behaviourist views of education are concerned with overt human behaviour, in the sense of observable action and activity. Note that behaviourism is not about getting pupils to behave well, but that it is concerned with broader aspects of human and animal behaviours. Strict, or classical, behaviourists downplay the role of mind and mental activity in learning, and are concerned with the observable behaviours that people exhibit.

> Behaviourists have no opinion or desire to understand internal mentalistic process but accept that the processes of reward and punishment associated with intrinsic factors influence behaviour as strongly as extrinsic, tangible rewards and punishments.
>
> (Woollard 2010: 7)

Learning is seen as involving a conditioned response to an external stimulus. 'The environment impinges on us, and we form associations about it in such a way that the more we are exposed to a particular environment, the stronger the association' (Strauss 2000: 34). What this means is that rewards and punishments (if not punishments *per se*, then at least the removal of rewards) are powerful motivators for learning: 'From this perspective, achievement in learning is often equated with the accumulation of skills and the memorization of information (facts) in a given domain' (James 2006: 54).

Experiments with animals have in the past formed a large component of behaviourist research. The classic example of this is Pavlov's experiment on conditioning with dogs. In this work, Pavlov started from the observed behaviour that when dogs detect food in their vicinity they will start to salivate. This process is known as 'stimulus-response'. Pavlov then made sounds which were presented at the same time as the food, bells, whistles, tuning forks and other sound sources being employed for this purpose. What Pavlov had done was to have 'conditioned' (key behaviourist term) the dogs to 'associate' (another important term) sound with food. After a period of such conditioning, the dogs would eventually salivate at the occurrence of the sound, without any food being present at all. This, behaviourists would say, is a conditioned response.

Later research including that of B.F. Skinner, one of the key figures in American behaviourism, involved animals learning to undertake desired behaviours, such as pushing a lever, and consequently being rewarded with food for a correct response, or punished if an incorrect response ensued, for example, with a mild electric shock. From this and similar research behaviourists concluded that rewards, which they called 'reinforcement', strengthen the likelihood of a desired behavioural outcome, while 'punishment' reduced the likelihood of an undesired behavioural outcome.

Although a number of facets of behaviourism are discounted in contemporary cognitive psychological accounts, nonetheless many aspects of it can be seen to exist in both schooling and learning. In schooling it can be seen in behavioural responses such as 'no running in corridors', 'walk on the left', 'stand up in assembly when the headteacher comes in'. In learning it can be seen in the division of complex tasks into smaller stages, in the sequenced acquisition of skills, and of repeating work, especially that which involves practical skills, which does not meet the required standard.

Cognitive and constructivist accounts

Although there are differences in emphasis between cognitive and constructivist accounts of learning, for our purposes we shall consider them jointly.

Unlike behaviourist approaches, cognitive theories of learning are interested in the action of the brain, and of particular interest here is the notion of *mind*. Constructivist accounts of learning are concerned with ways in which individuals construct meaning for themselves. Piaget believed that the way in which this was done was through the development of mental 'schema', which he saw as ways of storing knowledge which we as individuals use to interpret what is going on around us. As time passes, we develop these schema so that they become increasingly complex. A very young child, for example, may have a schema for the family car. This involves being strapped into a child seat and being taken places. As their experiences accumulate, they also become aware of notions of driving, of being filled up with fuel, of speed of movement, and so on. This schema is likely to link to other similar things – buses, trains, aeroplanes – and modified as appropriate.

For Piaget, learning involves 'assimilation' and 'accommodation'. Assimilation occurs when an individual encounters some new information. This will involve assimilating this new information into an existing schema. This will happen if the new information does not disagree with what the schema already contains. If there is something which seems to contradict the information in a schema, a black swan, for example, then the schema needs to be altered in order to be able to accommodate this new information. When there are no such contradictions present in an individual's mental representation of what is going on, then a state of equilibrium is said to exist; arriving at this state is referred to as 'equilibration'.

Constructivist accounts treat the individual learner as making meanings for themselves, and this has ramifications for the ways in which teaching and learning are considered:

> Learning is always an active process. The learner actively constructs her/his learning from the various inputs s/he receives. This implies that the learner needs to be active in order to learn effectively.

> Learning is about helping pupils construct their own meaning, not about 'getting the right answer', as pupils can be trained to get the right answer without actually understanding the concept.
>
> (Muijs and Reynolds 2005: 62)

One of the implications of this view of learning is that all of the learners in a given class will be actively constructing their own meanings during the course of a lesson. It may seem that this is entirely the case, and accords well with your experiences and that you agree that this is the case with the classes that you teach. What a constructivist view of education requires of you, the teacher, is to think about ways in which you can approach the learning of each pupil that you teach, and of how you can plan for personalization and differentiation. Remember, though, that constructivism is a view of learning, not teaching.

Socio-cultural accounts

Socio-cultural accounts place the learner as being acted upon by society, by interactions with others, including by socialization and socializing. One of the early researchers who promoted this view of development and learning was the Russian psychologist, Lev Vygotsky. He observed:

> Every function in the child's cultural development appears twice: first, on the social level, and later, on the individual level; first, between people (interpsychological) and then inside the child (intrapsychological). This applies equally to voluntary attention, to logical memory, and to the formation of concepts. All the higher functions originate as actual relationships between individuals.
>
> (Vygotsky 1978: 57)

What this means is that the child learns from others, and that the way that they function as an individual is derived from the ways in which they do this. One of Vygotsky's significant contributions to the way in which we view learning was his notion of the 'zone of proximal development' (ZPD).

The ZPD refers to the fact that individuals are able to work at a higher level when they doing things with other people than they would be able to do by themselves. Vygotsky described the ZPD as being: 'The distance between the actual development level as determined by independent problem solving and the level of potential development as determined through problem solving under adult guidance or in collaboration with more capable peers' (Vygotsky 1978: 86). In the case of school pupils, this is true when they are working with adults, or with other learners who are more experienced in some areas than they are themselves. As Vygotsky observed, 'We said that in collaboration the child can always do more than he [*sic*] can independently' (1978: 209). This has obvious implications for the ways in which we can consider learning taking place. It means that by undertaking fruitful collaborative work in class, such as groupwork and cooperative learning, these are contributing towards the development of the individual. This is important in a consideration of why group-work may be appropriate, because, as Vygotsky observed: 'what the child is able to do in collaboration today he will be able to do independently tomorrow' (1987: 211).

Scaffolding

Another aspect of socio-cultural learning theory is that of 'scaffolding'. The notion of scaffolding derives from the process of building. The scaffolding is required to prop up the house until it is sufficiently firm on its own foundations to stand by itself. Likewise in education, scaffolding occurs when a teacher, or significant other person, provides help, assistance and, crucially, support, to enable a learner to make progress. One of the main architects of the notion of scaffolding is Jerome Bruner (see Wood et al. 1976). He describes how the knowledge that the developing pupil is acquiring (or participating in) is supported by the teacher, who focuses them onto key points relating to the task in hand. As pupil learning becomes more secure, interventions made by the teacher are required less frequently, which means that scaffolding can be withdrawn in stages.

Communities of practice and situated learning

The principal idea behind situated learning is that learning is rooted in activity, it is situated in a context, and it does not involve the simple transmission model we discussed earlier. The learning act here is conceived in terms of the interaction between the learner and their environment, the learner with other individuals and, in addition, a societal processing of information. What this means is that learning takes place within a cultural context: 'learners inevitably participate in communities of practitioners and that mastery of knowledge and skill requires newcomers to move towards full participation in the socio-cultural practices of a community' (Lave and Wenger 1991: 29). Lave and Wenger describe how 'legitimate peripheral participation' (the subtitle of their 1991 book) moves learners from taking part 'on the edges', as it were, of what they describe as 'communities of practice', to more centralized positions as they progress along a novice–expert continuum. They describe these communities as being:

> . . . a set of relations among persons, activity, and world, over time, and in relation with other tangential and overlapping communities of practice. A community of practice is an intrinsic condition for the

existence of knowledge, not least because it provides the interpretive support necessary for making sense of its heritage. Thus, participation in the cultural practice in which any knowledge exists is an epistemological principle of learning.

(Lave and Wenger 1991: 98)

For our purposes in thinking about lesson planning, communities of practice can be seen as being an integral feature of the many ways in which teachers work. Schools do not tend to regard some activities as being solely the province of a gifted few. The whole class normally works at similar tasks at the same time as each other. An implication of participation in a community of practice is that all pupils can participate in the learning activities in which they are engaged, and that they all have something to contribute.

Acquiring and participating

Another interesting standpoint in considering knowledge and its learning, both in schools and beyond, is represented by the work of Anna Sfard, who distinguished between learning which we *acquire*, and learning in which we *participate* (Sfard 1998). This is an important and useful distinction for us to consider in our work on planning for learning in lessons, as these two metaphors for learning, as she refers to them, take us into quite specific ways of conceptualizing learning.

The notion of learning as the acquisition of knowledge is a straightforward one. We can readily see how this sits with both the complex ways we have been thinking about learning, and with the naïve theories and folk pedagogy of non-experts. In the acquisition metaphor, knowledge is treated rather like a commodity, something you can pick up, handle and own. You can acquire it in a not dissimilar fashion from going around a supermarket and placing things in your trolley. As Sfard observes: 'The idea of learning as gaining possession over some commodity has persisted in a wide spectrum of frameworks, from moderate to radical constructivism and then to interactionism and socio-cultural theories' (1998: 6). Indeed, describing learning as a process of acquiring knowledge tends to be the commonest way in which it is discussed.

In contrast to this is the notion of learning as something in which an individual participates. This is a rather more complex way of viewing learning. In it Sfard suggests that: 'the learner should be viewed as a person interested in participation in certain kinds of activities rather than in accumulating private possessions' (1998: 6). This can readily be applied to many forms of knowledge in schools which involve participation, but it also invokes the communities of practice idea from Lave and Wenger above. As James and Brown observe: 'Knowledge is not a thing to be possessed but a state of knowing, shared within a community of practice and expressed through activity' (2005: 13). This has clear resonances for many teachers across the spectrum of different age phases, different subjects on the curriculum and different types of schooling.

Having surveyed a range of theoretical accounts concerning learning, it is now time to turn our attention to a consideration of what teachers are able to do with this information, and what sorts of knowledge they themselves will require in order to effectively teach, and for pupils to effectively learn.

Pedagogical content knowledge

Knowing what there is to teach is different from knowing how to teach it. The American educational psychologist Lee Shulman distinguishes between the two by referring to the former as 'subject matter content knowledge', and the latter as 'pedagogical content knowledge'. He writes:

> Within the category of pedagogical content knowledge I include, for the most regularly taught topics in one's subject area, the most useful forms of representation of those ideas, the most powerful analogies, illustrations, examples, explanations, and demonstrations, in a word, the ways of representing and formulating the subject that make it comprehensible to others. Since there are no single, most powerful forms of representation, the teacher must have at hand a veritable armamentarium of alternative forms of representation, some of which derive from research whereas others originate in the wisdom of practice.
>
> Pedagogical content knowledge also includes an understanding of what makes the learning of specific topics easy or difficult: the conceptions and preconceptions that students of different ages and backgrounds bring with them to the learning of those most frequently taught topics and lessons. If those preconceptions are misconceptions, which they so often are, teachers need knowledge of the strategies most likely to be fruitful in reorganizing the understanding of learners, because those learners are unlikely to appear before them as blank slates.
>
> (Shulman 1986: 9)

This is another important distinction to make. It affects you, the teacher, because you will not only need to know what there is to be taught and learned, Shulman's subject matter content knowledge, but you will also need to know how to teach it. You will be developing a repertoire of pedagogical content knowledge (PCK). Initiating the development of PCK is the purpose of teacher training, but it does not stop there. Good teachers are continually adding to their stock of PCK. This includes ways to help learners understand what is required of them, and ways in which various topics can be taught so as to lead to learning. PCK is a component of what it is to be a teacher. An implication of Shulman's work is that having good subject matter content knowledge alone is not enough; PCK is also required in order for learning to take place in the pupils who are taught.

Combining theory with practice

Having considered theoretical accounts of learning and looked at the PCK, we now need to put these together to explain why a knowledge of both will have an impact upon the ways in which you plan for learning, and how this will actually affect the ways in which you plan for teaching. Let us take an example of this. The New Zealand education researcher John Hattie has noted:

> Every year I present lectures to teacher education students and find that they are already indoctrinated with the mantra 'constructivism good, direct instruction bad'. When I show them the results . . . they are stunned, and they often become angry at having been given an agreed set of truths and commandments against direct instruction.
>
> (2009: 204)

Hattie's description of 'direct instruction' involves a process of stages of delivery of a lesson. Clearly if you are following a principle such as this, then you will plan your lesson in order to fulfil the requirements of the model, and of the way you believe that learning should take place. As a sideline, it is worth noting that in this book we are not saying 'constructivism good, direct instruction bad', but what we are doing is recognizing that as schools, academies and colleges turn their attention more and more onto the minutiae of classroom learning, a number of differing approaches are likely to be needed.

Planning for learning – behaviourism

In planning for learning which uses a behaviourist approach, Woollard notes that: 'Behaviourist teaching is associated with learning that is contextualised, kinaesthetic, practical, visual, verbal and motivated. It is learning that is structured, sequenced, didactic, efficient and effective' (2010: 64). This means that the ways in which the teacher plans for learning in this fashion will involve sequencing, especially of skill acquisition. In order to do this there will be an overall learning programme, or scheme of work, which has detailed the order in which skills need to be developed. The teacher will use positive reinforcement in the form of praise, encouragement and grades in order to reinforce the desired responses. Learning will be assessed through the use of tests, often trying to measure skills in an ascending sequence of difficulty (although they may not be presented in this manner). Common behaviourist testing involves closed questions and timed unseen tests. Practice tests are used as preparation for the required behaviour in the high-stakes tests, the ones which count.

Some aspects of rote learning are also associated with behaviourism (Tulving and Craik 2000: 4), especially when enacted as drill and practice. Aspects of this can be seen in primary schools in whole class chanting of times tables, for example. The important thing for us here is that rote-learning should be seen as a precursor to understanding, which is different from learning. For example, a child may mentally recite their times table in order to arrive at the answer to the question 'what is five times nine?'. This behaviourists would see as a stimulus ('what is five times nine?') – response ('forty-five') matter. The goal in behaviourist modes of teaching would be to have such responses so well ingrained in the pupil that the stimulus question would elicit the response forthwith. What can happen in some instances is that the pupil has learned the times table as a sequence, and so can get to the answer only by working their way through the nine times table in order, starting from 'one nine is nine, two nines are eighteen'. Behaviourist approaches would address this by providing more practice test questions which were timed in such a way that there was enough time allowed for the respondent to do this.

Whether the child actually knows what this multiplication sum actually *means* in practical terms is the objective of teaching for understanding, which needs to build on remembering. There are disputes as to whether the role of remembering as the product of rote-learning is of itself sufficient, as we explore later in this chapter. The revision of Bloom's taxonomy, shown in Figure 1.5, places remembering on the base level of thinking skills, followed by under-standing. For your planning for learning there are clearly things you want the pupils to be able to remember, and so it might be that you put this into practice by using behaviourist approaches in the first instance.

Planning for learning – cognitive and constructivist

Planning for involving cognitive and constructivist approaches to learning requires the pupils to actively construct meanings for themselves. What this means for the teacher is that teaching according to this view of learning will involve the teacher in helping learners progress from being novices towards more expertise. It will entail dialogue, both between teacher and pupils, and pupils among themselves, in the use of formative assessment to develop pupils' structural learning, and of facilitating application of learning in novel situations.

Planning for learning – socio-cultural

Planning for learning according to socio-cultural accounts involves a consideration of the interaction between the individual and other people:

> Thinking is conducted through actions that alter the situation and the situation changes the thinking; the two constantly interact. Especially important is the notion that learning is a *mediated activity* in which cultural artefacts have a crucial role. These can be physical artefacts such as books and equipment but they can be symbolic tools such as language.
>
> (James and Lewis 2012: 192, original emphasis)

Planning for learning in this fashion will involve discussion, group-talk, tools and their use, activity, problem-solving and creative tasks.

Mixing them up

As should be apparent from these accounts, there are aspects of all of the theories we have been discussing in the ways that teaching and learning take place in the classroom. In considering your own pedagogy and planning for learning you may well use selections from all of them depending on the types of learning, activity and tasks you want the learners to engage with. The subjects you teach and the various topics within them can also have an effect. After all, if you are dealing with key health and safety issues you will not want the pupils to be employing discovery learning techniques! Views of learning will influence everything about your pedagogy from the way you organize the classroom to the way you choose activities. For example, if you wish to only engage in individuated instruction, your classroom will be arranged with the chairs and desks separated from each other, and all facing the front. If, on the other had, you wish to encourage learning through discussion, then you will arrange tables in groups so that this can take place.

Although rote-learning is making something of a comeback in some influential contemporary views of learning, it is not as yet the dominant modality, and may not become so. The notion of education being everything you can remember, but with no sense of understanding, is problematic. We want our current generation of pupils to be educated to understand. One frustration voiced by teachers is that they cannot understand on behalf of the learners. At this point it is useful to think about what it means to understand, and whether the necessary preliminary stages involving prior learning have been successfully assimilated:

> Lack of understanding leads to difficulty in remembering techniques since steps in arbitrary techniques are easily forgotten; missing steps

can only be repaired through testing out possibilities, but this development needs a base of understanding that allows evaluation of what is 'reasonable'. Lack of meaningfulness, therefore, in the long term, leads to faulty technique and lack of confidence, negative attitudes . . .

(Brown 2012: 105)

So though remembering is an important early stage in learning, it needs to be placed alongside understanding for it to be effective.

Deep learning

We are talking about learning here as though it were all the same, but this is not the case! One clear distinction that can be drawn is that between deep and shallow learning. As Ramsden observes, in deep learning there is an 'intention to understand' in which the 'student maintains the structure of the task', whereas in surface approaches to learning the objective is 'only to complete task requirements' (2003: 47). With the multiple testing regimes that UK school students undergo, shallow learning can also be characterized as learning in sufficient detail only to pass a test, which, once taken, can be soon forgotten. Learning of this sort is unlikely to be of use to pupils; it is deep learning we wish to foster, and it is deep learning that we are planning for. Knowledge of PCK helps here, but it is appropriate too for teachers to think about what happens to the learning that they ask pupils to engage with. At what points will it be revisited, developed and re-examined? These are points which we discuss in more depth in the section on long- and medium-term planning in this book.

Conclusions

So to return to lesson planning, the whole purpose of which is, as we have seen, to plan for *learning*, thinking about what sorts of theoretical accounts you will be employing in your lessons is not simply a matter of academic curiosity, it is key to your pupils developing their own understandings. Knowing that some learning benefits from direct instruction, whereas other learning requires practice, group work and the application of skills is highly relevant in the way you plan for, and enact, what you and the pupils will be doing. At its most extreme, for example, you would not employ a 'chalk and talk' session if the aim was for the pupils to play football; you could talk about it for hours, but the whole point is to let the pupils get out and kick the ball around, to participate in the learning activity.

Summary

This section has considered learning and its role in lesson planning. We have looked at knowledge and discussed how there are different types of knowledge, and that being aware of these is important when considering how best to plan. We have looked at differences between acquiring knowledge and participating in it. We have considered three key families of learning theory: behaviourism, cognitivism and socio-cultural accounts. We have explored why these are of more than academic interest, but affect the ways in which teaching and learning take place at a fundamental level. Pedagogical content knowledge is a crucial part of the intellectual make-up of the teacher, and we have seen how important this is, both in terms of how topics are taught, and also in the ways in which teachers think about teaching and learning. Finally we have considered the differences between rote-learning and understanding, and talked about how the latter is what is needed for contemporary education, as remembering alone is by itself an insufficient condition for deep learning to have occurred.

Reflective questions

- As you teach, think about which learning theory best accounts for what you are doing.
- What elements of behaviourism do you notice in and around school?
- What is your school's attitude to group work, if it has one? Why is this?
- Are there models of learning which are appropriate for some aspects of what you teach, but not others?
- Think actively about your own developing pedagogical content knowledge. How are you adding to this?

8 Assessment and lesson planning

Introduction

Assessment is a key issue in contemporary educational discourse. All aspects of the teaching and learning process hinge on assessment. Indeed, it is possible that some external commentators, such as government and media, view assessment as a proxy for education; in other words the quality of a school, and the quality of teaching and learning in it, are judged by how well the pupils do in terms of their assessment results.

In this chapter we look in detail at what is involved in classroom assessment, at how you, the teacher, are able to plan for and enact assessment, and at ways in which various types of assessment can be used in both everyday practice as well as in longer-term significant assessments.

Assessment terminologies

There are a number of terminologies concerning assessment which are used by teachers, schools, Ofsted, academics and many others. There can often be seen to be clear evidence of definition slip between various users. Let us start this chapter by looking at, and defining for our purposes, what the various commonly encountered words *actually* mean. We will start with one of the most frequently encountered distinctions, that which draws distinctions between 'formative' and 'summative' assessments.

Summative assessment

Summative assessment is in essence a way of *summarizing* the attainment of a pupil. It can also be referred to as assessment of learning (A of L) It involves marking, grading or levelling, and presenting the information from the assessment in a summarized fashion. Examples of summative assessment gradings include: level 5, GCSE grade B, A level grade C, degree classification 2i, Grade 4 piano, 100 metres swimming, driving test pass, and many others. What summative assessment is normally telling us is the attainment position of a pupil or group of pupils at a particular point in time. It does this by grouping those with similar attainments together, so that we know that a Grade C at GCSE should carry the same level of meaning whether it is in English, maths, art, PE, or any other subject.

Some assessments, the driving test being a good example, can be taken until they have been successfully passed, and in some schools modular examinations are treated in a similar way and persevered with until the student gets the desired grade, for example, GCSE grade C.

The examples of summative assessments given above are all varieties of what are normally referred to as 'high-stakes' examinations. These are ones which have some sort of currency in externally validated assessment regimes. However, not all forms of summative assessment are high stakes in nature. For example, many teachers will want to test their pupils during, or at the end of, a phase, stage, unit or other point in a scheme of work. These summative assessment tests will also be reduced to a summarized mark, examples including 6/10 (six out of ten), 60 per cent, level 4b, B+, or similar.

Undertaking summative assessments in this fashion means that it is possible to judge the performance of one learner against others in the cohort and beyond. It also means that an individual pupil can be judged against their own previous performance. This aspect of assessment, where an individual's personal progression is assessed, is referred to as 'ipsative' assessment. Summative assessment can also be used by teachers to try to establish the efficacy of learning in identified elements of a teaching and learning programme, as well as determining the level and degree that each individual pupil has attained.

Harlen and James described the essential characteristics of summative assessment as involving these aspects:

- It takes place at certain intervals when achievement has to be reported.
- It relates to progression in learning against public criteria.
- The results for different pupils may be combined for various purposes because they are based on the same criteria.
- It requires methods which are as reliable as possible without endangering validity.
- It requires some quality assurance procedures.
- It should be based on evidence from the full range of performance relevant to the criteria being used.

(1997: 373)

Formative assessment

Formative assessment can also be referred to as assessment for learning (AfL), and though it can be argued that there are differences between the two, for our purposes we will take them to be the same thing. Formative assessment refers to assessment which helps form what comes next in the teaching and learning cycle. It is assessment which is rooted in the moment, takes place in and during action, and helps steer the pupil towards the next stage of what they will be doing.

> Formative assessment is that process of appraising, judging or evaluating students' work or performance and using this to shape and improve their competence. In everyday classroom terms this means teachers using their judgements of children's knowledge or understanding to feed back into the teaching process and to determine for individual children whether to re-explain the task/concept, to give further practice on it, or move on to the next stage.
>
> (Tunstall and Gipps 1996: 389)

One of the important aspects of AfL is that it does not automatically involve grading or marking necessarily (although it can, as we shall see), but that it involves teacher and pupils in reflecting on work undertaken, and thinking of ways in which the work can be developed.

The relationship between formative and summative assessment

We have described formative and summative assessment as though they are entirely distinct and separate activities:

> It is sometimes difficult to avoid referring to these as if they were different forms or types of assessment. They are not. They are discussed separately only because they have different purposes; indeed the same information, gathered in the same way, would be called formative if it were used to help learning and teaching, or summative if it were not so utilized but only employed for recording and reporting. While there is a single clear use if assessment is to serve a formative purpose, in the case of summative assessment there are various ways in which the information about student achievement at a certain time is used.
>
> (Harlen 2005: 208)

This is important to note, and it is probably better to think of assessment between formative and summative as being on a continuum, from what might be termed pure formative assessment at one end, to pure summative assessment at the other. But these distinctions are probably not held as rigidly in schools where there can be confusions between what counts as formative assessment and what as summative. For our purposes we wish to be very clear with regard to such distinctions. Formative assessment is assessment which is carried out in the moment and is designed to help the learning process *as it takes place*. Formative assessment is *done with* the learner. Summative assessment takes place after the learning has occurred, and is designed to summarize what has been done so far. Summative assessment is *done to* the learner. These differences can be conveniently represented in diagrammatic form, as in Figure 8.1. Figure 8.1 also introduces another important assessment terminology, this being 'the formative use of summative assessment'. What happens here is that assessment results from tests, marks, grades and levels are used to inform the next stages in learning in which the pupils will be engaged. This gives rise to discussions with the learners along the lines of 'you are a level 4c now, I want you to be a level 4b next time'. Of course, whether such discussions are of any value is another matter, but it is important to note that so common is this way of working that in some schools it is referred to as though it were formative assessment proper – we want to be clear: it isn't!

Assessment data – what is it?

Discussions concerning grades and marks which have been awarded to pupils take us to another contested area of assessment discourse, and that is what is meant by the term 'assessment data'. The simplistic way of

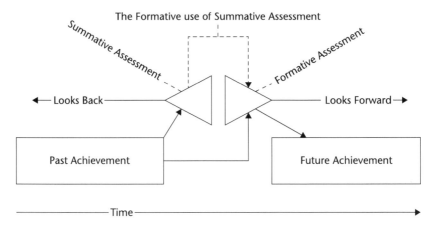

Figure 8.1 Formative and summative assessment.
Source: Fautley and Savage (2008: 27)

conceptualizing assessment data is to think that it is anything that is graded, marked or levelled, and then entered into a markbook, physical or electronic. But as Dylan Wiliam, a significant figure in the architecture of formative assessment observes, 'if formative assessment involves making marks on a piece of paper, or putting scores into a spreadsheet then you're doing it wrong' (2008: 9).

We have already observed that formative assessment takes place in the moment, and involves making judgements as work is progressing about what could and should be done next. What this means in practice for you, the teacher, is that sometimes formative assessment might not 'feel like you are doing assessment', as one teacher put it. The effect of this was observed by Ann Neesom: 'Teachers feel obliged to "prove that they are doing assessment", this is usually expressed in terms of having to write something down, for example, ticking boxes' (2000: 5). Formative assessment is not like this, instead it involves making on-the-hoof judgements about what is going on, and what you as the teacher need to do to the lesson while it is in progress in order to change tack, to develop learning or to correct misunderstandings. As the teacher above said, this may not feel like assessment, but it is! It is also, as Dylan Wiliam observed, unlikely to involve putting anything into a spreadsheet. Let us consider a couple of practical examples to help contextualize this.

Formative assessment vignette 1

A PE teacher is working with a group of pupils who are learning how to throw the discus. The teacher has demonstrated, modelled and talked about what she wants the pupils to focus on in this lesson, which involves posture and holding the discus properly. After a pupil has thrown the discus, the teacher says, 'Not bad, that was a level 4c throw, next time I want you to achieve a level 4b throw, please. Next pupil please.'

Formative assessment vignette 2

A music teacher is giving a group of pupils a guitar lesson. The focus of the lesson is correctly playing a melody which the pupils have been learning to play for a few weeks. After one pupil plays the guitar piece, the teacher says, 'Not bad, that was a level 3a performance, now I want you try to make it a level 4c please.'

Vignettes discussion

Clearly both of these examples are extremely unhelpful in their developmental potential for improving the pupils' learning in either case (though, sadly, also very real in terms of the ways some schools misinterpret assessment data use). What is far more likely to happen is that the PE teacher will comment on the actual throw of the pupil, pointing out what she wants the pupil to do, probably involving a slowed-down modelling or a very precise set of instructions which help that pupil specifically to be able to develop and improve their throw next time. The guitar teacher will do the same, pointing out, again probably re-modelling the precise details of what she wants the pupil to do, where to put her fingers on the guitar strings, and talking with the pupil to make sure that understanding what is required specifically for that pupil, in playing that piece of music, is made clear with regards to what needs to be done next.

Feedback

It should be obvious that what is important in each of these cases is the quality of the feedback that the teacher gives to the pupils. This is what will make a difference, this where learning takes place, and this is where improvement can be discussed, modelled, picked over, restructured if necessary, and taken on to the next stage. As Alastair Irons notes: 'Feedback is a key aspect in assessment and is fundamental in enabling students to learn from assessment. Helping students to learn from their activities is a key aspect of feedback – particularly through encouraging dialogue' (2007: 1–2).

This last point is an important one, feedback is a dialogue, not a teacher monologue! The points made need discussing with the learner to ensure that they have understood, they know what to do, and they understand what they need to do in order to make progress with their learning and consequently with their attainment too.

When feedback is used in this way, to influence the way that things will be done next, it is sometimes referred to as 'feedforward'. This terminology has been around for a while; it was used in the National Curriculum task group on assessment and testing (TGAT) report of 1988:

> Promoting children's learning is a principal aim of schools. Assessment lies at the heart of this process. It can provide a framework in which educational objectives may be set and pupils' progress charted and expressed. It can yield a basis for planning the next steps in response to children's needs . . . it should be an integral part of the educational process, continually providing both 'feedback' and 'feedforward'. It

therefore needs to be incorporated systematically into teaching strategies and practices at all levels.

(TGAT 1988: para 3)

Assessment data and feedback

We observed above that it is helpful to think of assessment as lying on a continuum between formative and summative. One of the implications of this will be that assessment data also lies on a continuum running alongside and parallel to this, with feedback in exclusively oral form being at one end, and feedback in exclusively written form at the other. A diagrammatic representation of this is shown in Figure 8.2. What this means is that assessment data has exclusively oral aspects at one end of this continuum. This can be problematic in some instances, as one of the issues with solely oral feedback is that it can be considered as being intangible, in that as it exists solely in spoken form, it can be difficult to recapture, replicate, or, in some cases, prove it existed at all! There is, however, little doubt that giving immediate oral feedback to learners is of significant benefit, and helps shape and influence work in the moment. As we move along the continuum the response given to work moves from being intangible to becoming increasingly tangible. Many teachers are finding ways to capture oral feedback to pupils, for example, by the pupils writing down a summarized form of what the teacher has been saying. Other teachers provide brief bullet points, and others use targets as formative feedback. At the other end of the continuum the assessment data, and the feedback associated with it, can exist in a very brief written format. For

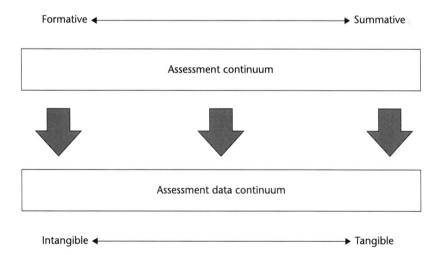

Figure 8.2 Assessment data and feedback.

example, results at degree, GCSE and A level can be expressed as simply a grade, with nothing by way of commentary available unless requested (and paid for!).

There is currently a drive in a number of schools to make all forms of feedback given to pupils tangible. In some schools this means that written feedback is the norm, whereas others have adopted more creative responses and teachers use spoken and recorded audio files to give feedback, while others video their comments. Although this drive towards increasing the tangible component of feedback is seemingly laudable, it should nonetheless be remembered that it is direct oral feedback, given in the heat of the moment while learning is actually taking place, that is likely to have the greatest influence on pupils. While tangible assessment data can clearly have a place in the evidence-bank you will use for planning future teaching and learning activities, the intangible should still have an important and useful role to play too.

Assessment data typologies

It has been observed that 'to teach is to assess' (Swanwick 1988: 149), and this will very much be the case when you are thinking about how assessment can inform your teaching. One of the starting points for ways in which this can be done is to list the various pieces of assessment data that you will need before starting to plan a unit of work or a lesson with it. See Table 8.1 for what such an assessment data list could include.

What is particularly apposite in thinking about this as assessment data is to simultaneously consider the issue of assessment evidence. In other words, how do you know the answers to these questions? As an example, these questions are rephrased in terms of evidence in Table 8.2.

Table 8.1 Assessment data

Knowing	Doing
What do the pupils know already?	What can the pupils do already?
Do they all know this?	Can they all do this?
If so, how well do they know it?	If so, how well can they do it?
What about those who struggle?	What about those who struggle?
What about those who find it easy?	What about those who find it easy?
Have they enough prior knowledge to be able to do it?	Have they acquired the necessary skills already?
How does this learning build on what they know already?	How does this activity build on what they can do already?

Table 8.2 Assessment evidence

Knowing	Doing
What evidence do I have to show that the pupils know already?	What evidence do I have to show that the pupils can do this already?
What evidence do I have to show that they all know this?	What evidence do I have to show that they can all do this?
What evidence do I have to show how well they know it?	What evidence do I have to show how well they can do it?
What evidence do I have about those who struggle?	What evidence do I have to show about those who struggle?
What evidence do I have about those who find it easy?	What evidence do I have about those who find it easy?
What evidence do I have to show they have enough prior knowledge to be able to do it?	What evidence do I have to show they have acquired the necessary skills already?
What evidence do I have to show how this learning builds on what they know already?	What evidence do I have to show how this activity builds on what they can do already?

This makes for a much stronger evidence base upon which to build lesson planning. It asks the key question 'how do I know?', and turns it into an evidential requirement. Although it is likely that you will know, or have an impression at least, thinking about assessment data in this way makes for a more powerful way of carrying out developmental planning. But how can you collect this data? This is where the various forms we have been discussing – formative assessment, the formative use of summative assessment, and summative assessment – come into play. You will have work that the pupils have done, you will have comments that you have made on their work, and you may well have marks, grades and levels awarded for the ways in which this work has been done by individuals within your classes. You will also have your reflections and lesson evaluations which you have been keeping concerning this work and your teaching of it. All of these contribute towards the evidence base we are discussing here. Using this sort of information in your planning is a logical development of Schön's (1983) notion of the reflective practitioner, and his discussions of 'reflection in action' and 'reflection on action', and builds on the discussions we had concerning reflection in Chapter 3 and elsewhere.

Success criteria

The notion of success criteria is one which can frequently be interchanged with assessment criteria. Using the term 'success' tends to render such criteria as being a positive aspect, as assessment criteria can carry negative connotations for some learners. In whatever fashion you choose to refer to them, or whether your school, college or academy has a preference, the important thing is to have thought about what these things are and what you will do with them.

In order to be able to develop the work that pupils are doing, one of the major changes you will be expecting is that their work will develop qualitatively over time, and that it will show increasing understanding of what quality involves. But how do they know this? One of the early writers on formative assessment made the observation that 'The essential conditions for improvement are that the student comes to hold a concept of quality roughly similar to that held by the teacher' (Sadler 1989: 121). In your planning for learning, one aspect of developing AfL that you will want to make clear is this one of pupil understanding of quality. One of the ways in which you can do this is by thinking about what the criteria for success in any given piece of work or task entail. But doing this is not easy, as Pirsig described:

> Quality – you know what it is, yet you don't know what it is. But that's self-contradictory. But some things are better than others, that is, they have more quality. But when you try to say what the quality is, apart from the things that have it, it all goes poof! There's nothing to talk about. But if you can't say what Quality is, how do you know what it is, or how do you know that it even exists? If no one knows what it is, then for all practical purposes it doesn't exist at all. But for all practical purposes it really does exist. What else are the grades based on?
>
> (1974: 178)

Knowing this, thinking about what quality is in whatever it is that your teaching and learning focus upon becomes a significant task. Simply saying 'because I said so' is not a good enough answer! So what are success criteria, and how can you use them in your planning? In order to begin to do this, let us first consider what a success or assessment criterion might look like. Table 8.3 gives a list of suitable characteristics that it is normally desirable that a success criterion possesses.

The purpose of Table 8.3 is to help with your teacherly thinking about what it is that is good, and has quality, in your teaching and learning. Hopefully it also goes some way towards dealing with Pirsig's issue mentioned above, that if you are not careful, when you try to define quality 'it all goes poof!'.

In order to produce such a list, the first stage in your thinking process will normally be to deconstruct the learning that the pupils will be doing, and produce a series of phrases which describe the ways that success will be achieved. Let us take as an example the teaching and learning from the formative assessment vignettes above to do this.

Table 8.3 Success criteria characteristics

A criterion should have a degree of exclusivity	It should, ideally, refer to a single, isolatable aspect of skill, knowledge or understanding
It should be specific enough to measure a single item/skill/construct without too many extraneous variables coming into play	As above, focusing on that singularity
A criterion should be assessable in some way	It should be possible to say how good something is, or that it exists or is absent
It should be possible to ascribe a rough valuing to the criterion	If it exists, how much of it is there? How good is it? Can a scale of value be produced? For example, poor, satisfactory, good, very good?
A criterion should have some relationship to the whole	It should be a deconstructed aspect of the total performance
It should not be evaluating an irrelevant aspect of accomplishment (such as one observation which was 'has tie done up'!)	Some things are peripheral. Are they really relevant to the performance in question?
A series of criteria which deconstruct a whole should, when taken together, go some way towards formation of an overall impression of the whole	The isolated deconstructed aspects of criteria should not simply be an amorphous mass of unrelated trivia, but should have an overall meaning
Just because something is hard to assess does not mean it should be ignored	Some things are easy to assess, but are they important?

Source: After Fautley 2010

The discus-throwing lesson involves a series of stages which the learners need to practise in order to move towards mastery. These include:

- holding the discus properly – correct position of fingers;
- stance and posture – moving in the most effective way;
- movement – achieving the required momentum before the throw;
- release – letting go at the appropriate time;
- aim – making sure the discus goes in the right direction.

Each of these can be turned into a success criterion in its own right, and, using the idea from Table 8.3 it should be possible to ascribe a rough value to this. To do this here we are here going to use a three-point scale, which accords to:

- – Not good enough
- = Meets the requirements
- + Exceeds the requirement

In these examples the three-point scale has been written with textual comments:

- Holds the discus properly: Good hold – Satisfactory hold – Poor hold
- Stance and posture: Good stance – Satisfactory stance – Poor stance
- Movement: Fluid movement – Secure movement – Restricted movement
- Release: Good release – Adequate release – Poor release
- Aim: Secure aim – Adequate aim – Poor aim

The guitar-playing lesson involves performing a melody, and again this can be deconstructed into a series of stages, which we will use a three-point scale to give value to:

- Uses left-hand fingers correctly: Accurately – Some errors – Lots of errors
- Right-hand technique: Secure – Adequate – Weak
- Musicality: Musical performance – Adequate performance – Poor performance
- Phrasing: Good – Adequate – Poor
- Stance and posture: Good stance – Satisfactory stance – Poor stance

To make this more manageable in the classroom, or on the field, the assessments could be presented in tick-box format, as seen in Table 8.4, for example. All the teacher has to do here is to tick the box; the text has been replaced by the shorthand '– = +'. Note that these symbols are a shorthand for the text, not a replacement for it.

In the guitar example there is an important success criterion which lies at the heart of quality, and relates to the item from Table 8.3 which states 'just because something is hard to assess does not mean it should be ignored'; this is the idea of it being a *musical* performance. This is what will lie at the heart of the guitar teacher's work, and why the pupil is presumably learning

Table 8.4   Assessments in tick-box format

	–	=	+
Holds the discus properly:			
Stance and posture:			
Movement:			
Release:			
Aim:			

to play the instrument in the first place. And yet it is much harder for a teacher to say 'that was a musical performance' than to note whether the pupil was using the right fingers. But assessing success this way is key to developing quality. Presumably the guitar teacher knows what a musical performance is when she hears one; she will use her professional judgement. Teachers should not be worried about doing this. If brain surgery involves making professional judgements – which it does – then teachers should not shy away from using them either.

Using assessment data in planning

Establishing what success involves is clearly an important part of planning for any teaching and learning. What is also needed is for the teacher to use this information over time to develop learning by building on the assessment data they have. What is important here is to use the full range of assessment data available to you, the teacher, from the classes you teach. We discuss throughout this book that it is important to have a long-term view of where learning should be, but that the short term, the lesson-by-lesson view, will need to evolve as a direct result of what has happened previously with each specific class. It is this information which will be used in planning lessons, as opposed to schemes or units of work.

To be truly formative, assessment data needs to inform both the *teaching* and *learning* processes. The teacher needs to learn from assessment data what it is that the pupils, or specific subsets or named individuals, cannot do to a base-level standard, and then address this in future learning episodes. Planning for learning is thus both a proactive and reactive phenomenon. What this means is that assessment data can be divided into three essential types. These are:

- **Day-to-day assessment** This is the type of assessment data which is of most use in the classroom, gives information which the teacher can use to plan future learning episodes. This type of assessment data will be of most use to the teacher when planning for the learning of each individual child.
- **Periodic assessment** This will take place occasionally, will be planned for as a separate event, maybe a test or assessment lesson. Its results can be used to inform the future direction of teaching and learning, but it also serves as an audit of learning.
- **Terminal assessment** This is assessment which occurs at the end of a unit, year, term, course, scheme of work, or other significant moment in the learning calendar. Some types are high-stakes assessments. They tend to be of limited developmental utility for individual learners, but are of high auditing potential.

An important aspect of this list is that it is a typology of assessment *data*, not of assessments. As we saw in the quotation from Wynne Harlen earlier in this chapter, 'the same information, gathered in the same way, would be called formative if it were used to help learning and teaching, or summative if it were not so utilized but only employed for recording and reporting' (Harlen 2005: 208). This is important to note in planning for learning, as it is important that as a teacher you do not accidentally confuse the auditing and developmental potential of assessment. Auditing occupies the national press, Ofsted and senior leadership teams, but can and should only occur as a result of good teaching and learning. Constant auditing alone is of little help, and the old country saying to the effect of 'weighing the pig every day doesn't make it fatter' is very true here. Assessment solely for auditing is like weighing the pig every day; you do have to feed it, or in our case teach it something, in between!

Who is the assessment data for?

This last point, the confusion between assessment for learning and auditing, brings us to an important question to be asked in thinking about planning for learning. This question is 'who is the assessment data for?'. From your perspective as a classroom teacher it is probably most helpful to consider three separate audiences for assessment data, and two essential uses. The audiences are the pupils, the teacher and what we might term 'the system', this being everything beyond the classroom, from the SLT through to league tables. The uses to which assessment data are put, again from a simplistic perspective, can either be to help learning and activity or to audit. A diagrammatic representation is shown in Figure 8.3.

What is important to bear in mind from a planning perspective is that the audiences shown in the second row of Figure 8.3 have very different requirements from each other with regard to the ways they will use assessment data. The pupils will want to know how well they have done, certainly, but will be active participants in formative assessment dialogues, and it is these which will help them in making progress. You, the teacher, will be using assessment data in planning for teaching and learning, but also in developmental auditing purposes. You will be wanting to know how, and how well, the pupils in your classes are progressing. This data, which includes that of the formative use of summative assessment, will be used by you to help with the planning and delivery of forthcoming lessons. The systemic requirements of your assessment data can be a little more opaque than the others, however. In many cases these can be more concerned with auditing purposes, and this data will have very little, if any, use in helping your pupils, in your classroom, improve in their learning. Knowing about the uses to which your assessment data will be put helps you to know how best to plan for implementation.

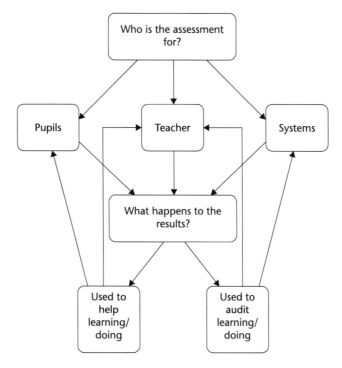

Figure 8.3   Who is the assessment for?
Source: Fautley (2010: 70)

Conclusion

So, having thought about these issues, how can you use assessment data to help in your planning?

One of the most important ways, but least obvious in evidential terms, is to use the information from the intangible end of the continuum we discussed earlier. Building on the ways you have interacted with the pupils is the surest way of ensuring that you tailor the planned learning to meet their needs. Moving to the more tangible aspects of assessment data, you can use the results of test scores to highlight where there may be gaps in learning and plan to remedy this. It is also pertinent to note that assessment data is not only there to highlight possible deficits in learning, it is also possible that the pupils have very thoroughly grasped key concepts, and so while going over things again may be relevant, there is also a point in moving on, and in finding other ways to build on their extant learning and knowledge in potentially more appropriate ways.

We hear a lot about evidence-based teaching, and it is in the use of assessment data in purposeful planning that this can be seen in your lessons. We have talked about day-to-day and periodic assessment, and it is in interpreting the results from these and using them in your planning that you will be personalizing learning for your pupils in a strategic fashion.

There is an all too present danger in the current climate of assuming that the only things that matter are assessment results and test scores. As we said in the opening of this chapter, what this means is that in some cases assessments have become a proxy for education, and that testing has become an end in itself. It is important for you to remember that you teach pupils, each of whom is a named individual, with a life-story and human baggage, and that it is what you do for them as people that matters, rather than how you deal with them as assessment statistics.

Summary

In this chapter we have considered the use of formative and summative assessment. We have thought about marking and grading, and discussed how it is through the proper and appropriate use of formative assessment – assessment for learning – that pupils are able to develop and their learning be moved on.

We have also discussed the notion of feedback and how it can be considered to lie on a continuum between the intangible and the tangible. The use of direct and immediate oral feedback as happening in the moment has been seen to be important, but least amenable to providing examples of detailed evidence, which SLTs in schools may require.

There are clear differences between day-to-day assessment and terminal high-stakes assessments, and it is in thinking about the day-to-day assessment that you will be making a real difference to learning. In a similar fashion, thinking about who precisely the audience is for your assessment data enables you to focus not only on presenting the right data for the right audience, but to consider what the most appropriate way of gathering such data is in the first instance.

Finally we have talked about the way that assessment data should, for the classroom teacher, be a means to an end, not an end in itself. Very few teachers go into teaching to generate data, most want to make a difference to young people's lives!

Reflective questions

- What do you understand to be the differences between formative and summative assessment? Is this how your school sees them too?

- What assessments do you have to do, and what assessments do you do because you wish to?
- How do you give feedback? Can this be worked on?
- What happens to any assessment data that you generate? Who else sees it?
- How do you use assessment data in your planning? Are there ways in which this could be improved?

9 Lesson, medium- and long-term planning

Introduction

For obvious reasons, this book has focused on the key topic of lesson planning. By now, we hope that you have got a firm grasp of our thinking and advice about how to plan for an individual lesson, how to enact that plan through an informed pedagogy, and how to reflect constructively on the plan – and its enactment within your teaching and your pupils' learning – through your evaluation.

In this chapter we are going to turn this bottom-up, individual lesson plan first planning process upside down. We are going to start with the notion of individual subjects and the knowledge, skills and understanding they contain, then consider longer-term plans which might encompass a Key Stage, and finally focus our attention on medium-term planning (which might cover a unit of work in a secondary school setting, or a week's work within a topic in a primary school setting). We will be widening our vision and looking at how an individual lesson plan is situated within these broader planning contexts. Along the way, we will be considering some broader themes about curriculum development and its relationship to your work as a teacher.

Looking beyond lesson planning

Each lesson that you teach does not exist in isolation. It relates to other lessons that you teach in a complex set of relationships. At the most basic level, any one lesson relates to the one that preceded it and the one that follows it. For this reason, it is a good idea to briefly signpost key activities and learning that have been undertaken in a previous lesson at the commencement of a new lesson; and at the end of the new lesson it is also a good idea to look ahead to what is to follow and try to create some forward momentum and curiosity about the learning that future lessons will contain in the pupils' minds. As we have discussed elsewhere, homework activities can help bridge the gaps between lessons too.

But there is another sense in which an individual lesson is situated more broadly within the lived experience of your pupils. Pupils 'receive' many lessons within one week. In the primary school, their classroom teacher may teach the vast majority of these; in the secondary school different teachers will teach specific lessons in each subject. Either way, the knowledge, skills and understanding that any one individual lesson contains will be contextualized by individual pupils within this weekly mix of teaching that they receive and the learning opportunities contained therein. For this reason, if nothing else, it is useful for you to consider how any one lesson that you are teaching relates to this broader milieu of experiences that your pupils will enjoy week by week.

Defining curriculum development

In this chapter, we are going to focus primarily on how any one individual lesson that you teach relates to the medium-term planning that this lesson is situated within, and then how this medium-term planning relates to a broader curriculum plan, or map, that might constitute a year's, or number of years', teaching and learning (perhaps within a Key Stage or part of a Key Stage). In doing so, we will be considering features of what is known as 'curriculum development'. So, before we get into the detail of units of work and what they might entail, it is worth considering what exactly is meant by this term – 'curriculum development'.

'Top-down' curriculum development

In common language use, we use the word curriculum to mean a set of arrangements for a course of study. It might include specific subjects, themes that span across subjects (e.g. globalization), specific ways of thinking or acting (e.g. creativity) or even ways of learning (e.g. visual, auditory and kinaesthetic). Curriculum development, therefore, is the process by which the content of a course of study is chosen, organized, structured and, to a certain extent, delivered.

Top-down approaches to curriculum development dominate our educational systems. Perhaps the most obvious example of a top-down structure of curriculum development in the United Kingdom is the National Curriculum. The 'National Curriculum' meant, until relatively recently, the over-arching structure of subjects and other elements that all state schools, regardless of their foundation or status, were required to provide as a core offering for all students. At the time of writing, there is a considerable amount of debate around the construction of a new National Curriculum to replace the previous version (which was implemented in 2007). The proposed new National Curriculum documentation is considerably shorter than the one it will replace. However, its brevity has not meant that debates around the content for each subject have been any less fierce. It has even led to some writers considering it more of a 'pub quiz' than an 'education' (Evans 2013).

But at the level of any one school, the National Curriculum as a top-down example of curriculum development is mitigated and mediated by decisions that headteachers and other senior staff might make about how to implement it within their own curriculum offering. The National Curriculum is, probably, one of several organizatory approaches that a school might utilize to help prepare a curriculum offering for their pupils. Within the primary school, staff may meet regularly to choose particular themes for a particular term's study (e.g. Ancient Egypt). Within that theme, the specific subject knowledge and content will be balanced and structured in different ways. Within the secondary school, the precise amount of curriculum time or financial resources that a particular subject receives are based on decisions made about the relative importance – or not – of that particular subject within the broader mix of subjects being included within a particular year or Key Stage. As schools have been given greater degrees of autonomy, the impact of the National Curriculum has waned, with academies and free schools being able to ignore it completely should they wish to do so. In light of this de-nationalization of the National Curriculum, it is interesting for you to consider what alternative organizing principles for curriculum development have been employed within your school or may be in the process of being considered in light of your school's greater degree of autonomy in this area.

At Key Stages 2 and 4, key accountability measures such as SATS and GCSE examinations could be considered to be another top-down form of curriculum development. In most primary schools, for example, the teaching of numeracy and literacy is often dealt with separately from the general topic work within which other subject knowledge is presented. Within the context of specific GCSE specifications, the accusation is often made that teachers 'teach to the test' (and this could be taken to be a good or a bad thing!). In both cases, the key content of the examination (or accountability) framework, in terms of knowledge and understanding, does influence the choices that are made in terms of how the medium- and longer-term planning are constructed at an individual school level.

However, these forms of top-down curriculum development, while important, are not the only way in which the term 'curriculum development' can be conceptualized.

'Bottom-up' curriculum development

While 'top-down' approaches to curriculum development dominate most educational thinking in our society, others have taken a more reflective view of the term 'curriculum'. Like Lawrence Stenhouse, we have found it helpful to position it alongside the work of the teacher. An over-emphasis on the external dimensions of the 'curriculum' as a set of subjects, themes and ways of thinking or learning can lead to what could be considered as an unhelpful over-objectification of the curriculum itself.

Stenhouse worried that the term 'curriculum' had been removed from the day-to-day remit of teachers and been taken over by politicians, examination providers and others. This, he argued, led to the teacher being seen as a disempowered labourer, being told what to do, where to do it and, increasingly, how to do it too. More prosaically, this concept of the term curriculum, he argued: 'rests on an acceptance of the teacher as a kind of intellectual navvy. An objectives based curriculum is like a site-plan, simplified so that people know exactly where to dig their trenches without having to know why' (Stenhouse 1980: 85). For Stenhouse, such a definition of the word 'curriculum' and the resulting imposition of centralized prescriptions of GCSE specifications or national curricula as a form of 'curriculum development' de-professionalized teachers and undermined their work. Throughout his career he developed alternative ideas that reasserted the teacher's role in curriculum planning and development. If, as he wrote, 'it seems odd to minimise the use of the most expensive resource in the school' (Stenhouse 1975: 24), it would be better, he argued, to 'reinvest in the teacher and to construct the curriculum in ways that would enhance teachers' understanding and capability' (Ruddock 1995: 5).

For Stenhouse, and us, teachers are central to the creation and delivery of a curriculum for their pupils. In this philosophical sense, you embody the curriculum that you deliver; as a teacher you 'enact' the curriculum through your teaching day by day. It is ideas such as this that led Stenhouse to make one of his most famous statements, that there is 'no curriculum development without teacher development' (Silbeck 1983: 12).

A pragmatic approach to curriculum development

As we have discussed in this section on curriculum development, the curriculum can be understood in varying ways. From the simple notion of it being a collection of subjects that are taught in a systematic way, to the philosophical and conceptual relocation of the curriculum to the pedagogy of individual teachers, it is vital that all of us who care about education do not allow the 'curriculum' to be hijacked by our politicians.

Pragmatically, whatever the politics surrounding the imposition of national curricula frameworks or examination specifications, there is always going to be a mixture of top-down and bottom-up approaches to curriculum development in our schools. As a teacher, you are not going to be left completely on your own to design and implement your own curriculum. Working collegiately in your departments or, in smaller schools as a whole staff, is a vital way of ensuring that your own work is situated within, and informed by, your school's vision for the curriculum that pupils will enjoy. In terms of how you design and implement medium-term planning (week by week) and longer-term planning (across a year or Key Stage), you will have to consider the broader curriculum frameworks within which your work is situated. However, this does not mean that you are a powerless individual. As a classroom teacher, you have a massive amount of influence to design and implement a curriculum that can impact on your pupils' lives in powerful ways. This influence and power need to be exercised responsibly. So, where do you start and how do you go about designing a curriculum within your own particular area of responsibility?

Turning lesson planning upside down: start with the subject

In most schools, subjects are the individual buildings blocks of the curriculum. Whether in primary or secondary schools, the notion of the individual subject, the key knowledge, skills or learning processes and understanding that each subject contains, and the development of your skilful pedagogy in introducing pupils to a particular subject, are all self-evident and often unquestionable.

The love of a particular subject is one of the key reasons that new teachers cite for wanting to learn to teach. For many of us, our academic subject was our 'first love' and something that we treasure very dearly. And therein lies a problem. The nature, culture and tradition of 'subjects' can lead to difficulties: 'School subject communities are neither harmonious nor homogeneous and members do not necessarily share particular values, subject definitions and interests' (Jephcote and Davies 2007: 210). Every subject that is represented within our schools has a particular culture that underpins it. This culture informs the 'identifiable structures which are visibly expressed through classroom organisation and pedagogical styles' (Goodson and Mangen 1997: 120). A subject's culture is what makes it unique and, in a simple way, helps pupils sense that they are studying a particular subject at a specific moment in the school day, whether that is in a subject lesson within a secondary school, or within a particular topic in the primary school classroom. It is important to recognize that a subject's culture goes beyond its knowledge. It also incorporates ways of thinking, acting and being, that inform those processes by which you may teach and your pupils learn.

For any structured process of curriculum development that is focusing on long-term planning, our advice is to start with your subject. For those of you teaching in secondary schools this will be easy in that the vast majority of your teaching will be in one main subject area; for those teaching in primary schools you will need to consider each subject area in turn at this deep level, as well as considering how these may interrelate and overlap. In the primary school particularly, collegial ways of working will help you share individual teachers' particular subject expertise within this planning process. No one is expected to be a subject expert in every area!

For us, the key process is to think through, at the highest level, what it is that your subject considers to be the most important set of ideas or principles that pupils should engage with throughout their formal school-based education. You can do this in a number of ways:

1   Reflect on your own experience as a learner within that subject's community. What have you learnt and valued over the years? Which teachers, or others, inspired and motivated you? How did they do it?

2   Engage with the various subject communities that work within education settings. Groups like the Historical Association or the National Association for the Teaching of English will all have their own sets of ideas about what should constitute a formal set of knowledge in their particular curriculum areas. These can be very useful prompts for your own thinking.

3   Examine the work of professionals within your particular subject field(s). Talk to them and ask them which areas of knowledge or sets of skills are particularly important for their work and how these have changed over the years.

4   Take note of the various curriculum frameworks such as the National Curriculum or appropriate examination specifications. However, please remember that these should not be the sole source of information for your work in this vital area. But you will have to reference your work to these at a basic level.

This type of reflective and consultative process does take time. But it is time well spent particularly when you are really trying to define, in detail, what it is that it is intrinsically important about a subject and how it ought to be taught. By way of an example, both of us have been music teachers at previous points in our careers. What was so important about music that makes us think, as music educators, that it ought to be taught to all children in our schools?

Well, first, there were helpful statements in the National Curriculum documentation. Statements such as this:

> Music is a unique form of communication that can change the way pupils feel, think and act. Music forms part of an individual's identity and positive interaction with music can develop pupils' competence as learners and increase their self-esteem. Music brings together intellect and feeling and enables personal expression, reflection and emotional development. As an integral part of culture, past and

present, music helps pupils understand themselves, relate to others and develop their cultural understanding, forging important links between home, school and the wider world.

Music education encourages active involvement in different forms of music-making, both individual and communal, helping to develop a sense of group identity and togetherness. Music can influence pupils' development in and out of school by fostering personal development and maturity, creating a sense of achievement and self-worth, and increasing pupils' ability to work with others in a group context. Music learning develops pupils' critical skills: their ability to listen, to appreciate a wide variety of music, and to make judgements about musical quality. It also increases self-discipline, creativity, aesthetic sensitivity and fulfilment.

(DES 2013)

Looking beyond the National Curriculum, various different subject associations that work within the field of music education had specific things to say about music and its importance. Finally, various individuals that we had met working as professional musicians and composers helped shape our thinking about what was intrinsically important about music as a subject culture, and how it could be presented in our curriculum planning (Savage 2005).

Starting with a subject is all about thinking big! The themes, topics, key knowledge areas and learning processes that you identify through this process are vitally important in helping you structure your long-term and medium-term planning. What is the best mechanism for doing this? Diana Burton suggests building up a conceptual hierarchy of ideas within a subject, and drawing a 'mind map' that shows the links between the various ideas, skills and topics that you identify (2005: 252). By doing this systematically you will get important insights into how you can sequence learning and plan for developing knowledge, skills and concepts over time. It will also show where these can usefully be introduced, and where reinforcement and development can take place so that skills can be worked at and concepts enhanced. This is the whole purpose of long- and medium-term planning. It is to these topics that we will now turn our attention.

The long- and medium-term plan

Having started with your subject(s), you will need to consider how to implement your ideas drawn from your reflections, readings and conversations into longer-term and medium-term planning. In this section we will present a structured process that will help you develop a long- and medium-term plan that supports the development of your pupils' learning in a coherent way. It does this through a simple, two-stage model built around the concepts of a 'curriculum map overview' and a 'unit map', for developing individual units of work.

Stage one: developing a curriculum map overview

Drawing on your work from your subject analysis, a curriculum map overview provides you with an opportunity to sketch out a long-term plan for a particular Key Stage. Figure 9.1 shows an example drawn from the work of one primary school at Key Stage 2.

On one side of A4 paper, Figure 9.1 provides a snapshot of learning for one year group within the Key Stage 2 curriculum. It contains the following basic elements:

1 a term-by-term representation of the various topics or themes contained within the year;
2 a breakdown of the basic content within each unit of work (through a short purpose statement, the key learning challenges and chosen pedagogical strategies);
3 a subject-by-subject breakdown where the specific contributions of each subject area can be identified. These will often contain references to the National Curriculum programmes of study for the relevant subject area.

Figure 9.2 shows an exemplar planning form from the work of a secondary school music teacher. In this, the curriculum overview map allows you to represent the key topics in your subject throughout a Key Stage. Alongside the titles of each unit of work, a brief description of purpose for each unit, the main learning objectives and pedagogical strategies can be outlined. As with the primary school example (Figure 9.1), key reference statements (in this example, key concepts) drawn from the National Curriculum programme of study are included.

Conciseness is the key here. You will want to keep your responses within each of the boxes very focused. This is not the time or place for extended expositions of, or justifications for, your chosen topics and other responses. But while conciseness is key, the work that goes into this document to ensure that progress and development are planned for and systematic is considerable and will take a lot of careful thought.

Development, in psychological terms, refers to the ways in which people mature cognitively. One of the key questions that you will want to consider in relation to your curriculum map overview is 'how does it allow for and facilitate pupils' cognitive development over time?' We can both remember a time when resource books of lesson materials used to say things like 'these units can be taught in any order'. This is not acceptable any more. During the course of

Subject Coverage by Cohort

Year 4		Team 1	Team 2	Team 3
	Key Topics			
	Purpose			
	Key Learning Challenges			
	Specific pedagogies			

Literacy Units	Numeracy Units	Science	ICT	RE
PE	Music	Art	PSHE	Design Technology

Figure 9.1 Exemplar curriculum map overview (primary).

Year	Unit of Work	Term 1	Term 2	Term 3	Term 4	Term 5	Term 6
7	Unit Title						
	Purpose						
	Key Learning						
	Key Pedagogy						
8	Unit Title						
	Purpose						
	Key Learning						
	Key Pedagogy						
9	Unit Title						
	Purpose						
	Key Learning						
	Key Pedagogy						

Key concepts:

Integrating Musical Processes
How will pupils develop their understanding of the music? (How)

Cultural Awareness
What is the music you want to explore? (Music studied) What is the music for? (Purpose)

Critical Thinking
What do you want the pupils to learn about this music? (Key Learning)

Being Creative
Where are the places we can develop creativity? Are there opportunities to work with other areas?

Communicating
Are there areas to incorporate expression through music?

Figure 9.2 Exemplar planning form for music (secondary).

a Key Stage, pupils' learning should develop and the pathways along which it develops are well known and generally understood. These need to be built into your own long-term planning.

So, when you are considering the completion of a curriculum map overview in a chosen subject area or for a particular year group, as well as the sequence of topics that you will include in each year you will want to consider the breadth and depth of learning that each unit might entail. You may want to give breadth to certain units of work, perhaps to ensure a blend of content across a year, but you will also want to study some key content within specific units in greater depth – and perhaps even revisit this key content within different units of work. This will require you to have a sound overview of the curriculum requirements of your topic area. To elaborate:

- Certain key concepts, skills, and knowledge may be introduced in one unit, at an early point in the year, and then be revisited and built upon later on (in another unit later in the year). The notion of the spiral curriculum is a useful one to consider in relation to this discussion about breadth and depth. There are many topic areas which can be usefully taught to younger children, but which can also be studied in greater depth in higher education settings. In the school context, having a spiral curriculum in mind when planning your curriculum map can allow you to introduce the essential features of a topic area at an early stage, and then revisit them in more depth later on in the year, or perhaps in the following year.
- Specific key concepts, skills or knowledge may depend on pupils understanding a prior set of concepts, skills or knowledge. Therefore, sequencing concepts, skills or knowledge is extremely important to ensure that pupils are not asked to do something cognitively complex without the basic cognitive skills being firmly established in their prior work. In many respects this is more complicated than it sounds, as any one individual pupil's learning may not be the same as another pupil's! You will need to ensure that your planning, even at this level, is appropriately differentiated. Similarly, we know that learning itself is seldom static or uni-directional (otherwise we would tell a pupil something once and they'd remember it for ever!) and tends to follow complex patterns that are difficult to plan for systematically. For this reason, a long-term curriculum plan, like any planning document, is just a plan and should not be stuck to religiously. Like your lesson planning processes, it should be reflected upon and evaluated regularly in light of the delivery of the curriculum during each term or year. It is vitally important to remember that your classes are full of individual pupils who will have their own particular idiosyncrasies and will learn differently from the class you taught in the previous

year. We would not expect your lesson planning and medium- or long-term planning to be identical each year (even though there may be similar elements contained within it).

Having started with your subject, identified key areas of knowledge, concepts and skills, and worked towards completing your curriculum map overview, it is time to turn our focus to the next level of planning – the medium-term plan. For most teachers, medium-term planning involves the writing of individual units of work.

Stage two: mapping the individual unit of work

When talking about a 'unit of work', we are referring to a subdivision of the curriculum map overview. In most schools, primary or secondary, this will refer to a term, or half a term's, work. However, in the primary school this may refer to a particular topic (within which different subjects are combined together) while within the secondary school this will probably refer to one discrete subject and the sequence of lessons within that subject.

Whatever context you are working within, mapping the individual unit of work is a useful exercise to undertake prior to writing the actual unit of work documentation (of which more below). This second phase of mapping helps to refine individual units of work within the whole curriculum map and consider whether they are placed appropriately to facilitate and evidence pupils' understanding. To do this mapping, select one of the topics or themes that you have included within your curriculum map overview and work through the following four steps using Figure 9.3 (the unit map).

1   Place the topic title in the middle of the unit map. For our example, we have taken the topic of gospel music.
2   Surround the topic title with the top level, key concept ideas drawn from your reflections and investigations into your particular subject area (discussed earlier). In the example we have provided, we have included five example concepts drawn from an analysis we did of music, as a subject area, and the various key informants that we considered the most important.
3   For each key concept area that you have identified (and which you have placed around your topic title), identify and consider some key questions that relate to that particular concept and how you seek to explore it within that specific unit. We have provided some example questions that you could adapt, but the key point here is that the questions that you write will help you explore the key concept ideas drawn from your own subject area within the context of your chosen unit of work.

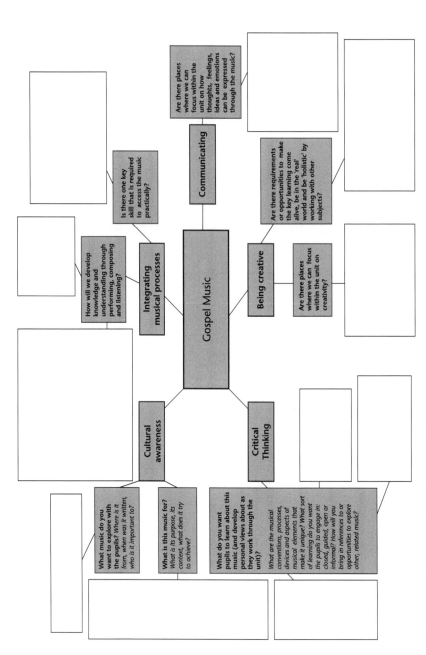

Figure 9.3 Exemplar unit map (secondary).

Are there places where we can focus within the unit on how thoughts, feelings, ideas and emotions can be expressed through the music?

Is there one key skill that is required to access the music practically?

Communicating

How will we develop knowledge and understanding through performing, composing and listening?

Integrating musical processes

Are there requirements or opportunities to make the key learning come alive, be in the 'real' world and be 'holistic' by working with other subjects?

Gospel Music

Being creative

Are there places where we can focus within the unit on creativity?

Cultural awareness

Critical Thinking

What music do you want to explore with the pupils? Where is it from, when was it written, who is it important to?

What is this music for? What is its purpose, its context, what does it try to achieve?

What do you want pupils to learn about this music (and develop personal views about as they work through the unit)?

What are the musical conventions, processes, devices and aspects of musical elements that make it unique? What sort of learning do you want the pupils to engage in: closed, guided, open or informal? How will you bring in references to or opportunities to explore other, related music?

4   Begin the process of answering your questions in the final part of the unit map. Be succinct and concise. Your answers here will help you write your own unit of work document.

Having a clear conception of how pupils will progress and develop through a Key Stage allows you to devise compelling learning experiences within units of work that are engaging and purposeful and help pupils develop their knowledge, skills and understanding within a particular subject area, or through a combination of subject areas within a particular theme. This chapter has presented a two-staged mapping process which started with an overview of the curriculum as a whole and then related individual units of work to this through a consideration of the key concepts and ideas. It has emphasized that it is helpful to build links between different topics, ensure a range of coverage and an appropriate blend of learning activities and pedagogical approaches. By placing the curriculum map overview at the centre of planning we have emphasized the importance of a balanced, rich and relevant curriculum to enable our learners to enjoy their experiences with us. The advantage of the planning tool is that the whole curriculum picture can be seen on a couple of pages. This gives you a clear map of where you are taking the pupils on their learning journeys.

Stage three: writing the unit of work

The unit of work is the final stage in the medium-term planning process. While lesson plans detail the learning objectives, teaching activities, resources, assessment and differentiation strategies for the individual lesson, the unit of work document provides an overview of the sequence of lessons that constitute a particular topic within your overall curriculum map. Units of work are sometimes referred to as 'schemes of work'. There are numerous exemplar documents for these documents available online. Some of the best ones tend to be short and concise, perhaps containing a one-page overview of the unit, followed by more details, including a short summary outline guide of the various lessons that the unit contains. Figure 9.4 illustrates one example of this from a primary school teacher's work. It is intended as an example of this sort of planning document, the text in a smaller font in the right-hand columns being intended simply as a guide to give some ideas concerning the materials that will be taught.

Specifically, a unit of work normally contains the following:

1   A title that is brief, concise and describes the unit of work. You can take this from your unit map and transfer it to your unit of work template.
2   A broad description of the unit of work, the key content or themes, and where it sits within the broader long-term plan for the Key Stage within which it is placed. Refer back to your curriculum overview map

Unit of Work	Spring Term	Year 3 & 4	2012/13
Area of Learning	Ancient Egyptians		
Learning Challenge 1	How did the Ancient Egyptians communicate?		
Learning Challenge 2	Who were the Ancient Egyptians?		
Learning Challenge 3	Can I make a Pyramid?		
Communication, Language & Literacy	Mystery and Adventure		
Mathematics	Counting, partitioning and calculating Securing number facts, understanding shapes Handling data and measures		
ICT	Research skills using the Internet Data handling–using tables and charts		
Physical Development	Dance – walk like an Egyptian Games – invasion games – hockey		
PSE (SEAL)	Going for goals		
RE	Parables		
Trips, Visits, Visitors, Special Days			

Prime Learning Challenge	How were the Ancient Egyptians buried?		
Subject Areas	WOW! Story of Tutankhamen & images of mummies	Children's Prior Knowledge & Questions	
	Learning Challenges (Questions)	Knowledge, Skills & Understanding (NC)	Outcomes
Week 1	Who was Tutankhamen?	Learn about features, ideas & beliefs of societies/people in the past (History 2a) Talk about what info they need and how they can find and use it (ICT 1a)	Children can imagine they have been asked to catalogue Tutankhamen's treasures for the National Egyptian Museum. Each item will need a picture, a short description and, where known, its use. To choose 4–5 items each using the Internet and books.
Week 2			
Week 3			
Week 4			
Week 5			

Figure 9.4 Exemplar unit of work (primary).

at this point and provide a simple explanation of how this unit of work fits within the overall plan for the Key Stage (i.e. why is it where it is?).

3   A set of learning objectives (in Figure 9.4 these are called 'learning challenges') for the whole unit, from which the learning objectives for individual lessons can be drawn. They can also give an indication of any prior learning that pupils should have achieved prior to commencing this particular unit of work. Significant details can be drawn from your unit map to help you form these learning objectives. You may want to pick up on key words from the subject-related key concepts that have informed your planning on the unit map, as well as the answers that you gave to the questions you defined within the unit map.

4   An outline of how much time is available for the unit. This would include lesson time (i.e. how many lessons are within the unit, how long each lesson is, etc.) as well as any homework time that might be assigned to the unit.

5   Key resources for the unit, including any specific pieces of information and communication technologies (ICT) that the unit might feature, any published resources that might be used, any artefacts or other objects that you will need access to, and key online resources (e.g. websites or other interactive resources) that you will need to utilize.

6   A broad description of any assessment, personalization or differentiation strategies that will be used throughout the unit. These should be general, not specific to individual lessons, and should highlight any innovative approaches or specific assessment requirements (i.e. those related to the National Curriculum or examination specifications if appropriate).

7   A list of the individual lessons within the unit of work, together with one or two sentences describing each one, key knowledge and skills covered and the expected outcomes. The unit of work should present an overview of these lessons (i.e. not detailed content) so that anyone reading the unit of work gets a general feel for the flow of lessons throughout the unit. Please keep this concise. This is not the time to write another bunch of lesson plans!

8   General statements related to the other curriculum links, e.g. cross-curricular links, extension and enrichment strategies, future learning (i.e. what the unit of work leads into) and key vocabulary.

In a secondary school setting, units of work are often written by heads of department for their curriculum team. In the primary school setting, these units of work documents are often written by teachers with a specific responsibility for a year group across the school. In either case, individual teachers may find themselves delivering a unit of work written by someone else. It is important to remember that these documents are there to serve as a guide to your own individual lesson planning and subsequent teaching. There will be many different ways that a unit of work can be delivered. How you plan your individual lessons within a unit of work depends on a range of factors, of which the general coverage provided by the unit of work is just one important factor. So, consider the unit of work as a map of the terrain. How you move the students from point A to point B is still your responsibility!

More generally, all teachers are responsible for creating a sense of direction, purpose and flow between their lessons. The unit of work document can help provide that formal framework for teaching. But pedagogical strategies such as providing summaries of learning through plenaries, highlighting or signposting future learning opportunities; using homework opportunities to establish links between lessons; and much more are equally important. As with the lesson plan, the unit of work planning process is something that you will need to bring to life within your teaching! Otherwise, it just remains a paper exercise that will only serve to frustrate you. Remember, the 'holy trinity' of planning, teaching and evaluation is as important here as it is within the individual lesson planning that you undertake.

Summary

In this section we have considered how lesson planning needs to fit within an overall structure of medium- and long-term planning. We have considered both 'top-down' and 'bottom-up' approaches to curriculum development. We have considered the place of knowledge in a longer scale time frame, and how planning for learning over a period of years, or within a Key Stage, is necessary in order to try to establish a 'big picture' view of teaching and learning. We looked in some detail at the notion of curriculum mapping, and at how this helps with both progression and development. We considered the ways in which concepts, skills and understanding develop over time, and how sequencing them correctly is vital when thinking about planning in the medium and long term. We looked at how units of work fit into such plans, and how the individual lesson plan then derives from this.

Reflective questions

- Does your school have to adhere to the National Curriculum? If not, how does it diverge?
- How are long- and medium-term planning laid out in your context?

- How involved are you with understanding how long- and medium-term planning take place?
- Do you have a view of the 'big picture' into which your individual lessons slot?
- Have you thought about curriculum mapping?

10 Differences in planning in the primary and secondary school

In the previous chapter we considered how the individual lesson plan itself is located within a broader set of planning materials, often referred to as medium- and long-term planning, and how these can be developed in different ways within the primary and secondary school. We identified one common element, the notion of the individual subject, which underpins planning in both settings. Whether you are planning to work as a primary or secondary school teacher, we encouraged you to start with the subject itself and use that as a springboard from which your long-term and medium-term plans emerge.

In our preparation for this book, we have spoken to teachers from many different schools about their planning. This has been a tremendously helpful and interesting experience. While both of us enjoyed careers as high school teachers of music, we have been struck by the significant similarities in planning that colleagues in primary and secondary schools have to consider. In both settings, teachers are required to write clear learning objectives, build engaging teaching activities, implement strategies for differentiation and assessment, as well as evaluate their work.

But obviously there are differences in approach to the organization and delivery of education that cast an interesting light on how teaching and learning are planned in the different school environments. The aim of this chapter is to explore some of these and, by doing so, to help you think a little differently about how you go about planning lessons within your particular school context. In the following chapter we will be looking at some of the common documentation and frameworks that teachers use in different settings. Here, we will start with some of the most obvious differences between primary and secondary schools and work our way down to some of the finer details and how they impact on the discrete elements of lesson planning. In particular, we will introduce two short case studies, one from a primary and one from a secondary school, to illustrate some of the lessons that teachers in both settings could learn from each other.

The structure and organization of the school

One of the most significant differences between primary and secondary schools is the number of pupils that they cater for! A typical secondary school has around 1100 pupils; an average primary school around 200 pupils (DfE 2010).

Although most schools, primary or secondary, place their pupils in groups of various kinds (e.g. form groups, mixed ability classes or ability sets), the notion of a 'class' is very different in each setting. Primary school children are generally taught in one class group throughout each day; secondary school children, although placed in a form group, work in any number of different class groups depending on the curriculum arrangements and policies.

The consequences of this are that a typical secondary school teacher will normally work with hundreds of different pupils each week; the primary school teacher will generally work with the same 25 and 30 pupils each day. The average time that each secondary school teacher spends with any one pupil is also significantly less than their primary colleagues. As we will see, this has a significant impact on all aspects of planning including the ability to differentiate effectively for individual pupils.

The structure of the curriculum

As we explored briefly in the previous chapter, the overarching curriculum structures for the early years and Key Stages 1 and 2 are different from those at Key Stage 3 and the GCSE and GCE examination specifications that frame teachers' work at Key Stages 4 and 5. The way that an individual subject is located within the curriculum structure varies immensely and the consequent effects of this on staffing, subject expertise and planning are considerable.

Within the primary school, key subject areas such as literacy, numeracy and science are often planned for and taught as specific areas; however, other foundation subjects (e.g. those covered within the National Curriculum) are often planned for and taught within topic areas (as we discussed in Chapter 9). In the average secondary school, the vast majority of lessons are taught in subject areas, with only occasional topic-based approaches being adopted for specific days or events. Despite one or two exceptions to this that we will explore in the second case study below, this is by far the norm for the majority of secondary school teachers.

From the perspective of the secondary school pupil, the organization of the school, in both its physical layout, staffing and curriculum organization, serves to differentiate between subjects in a very rigid way. Geography is taught in one place by Miss Jones; mathematics is taught in another place by Mr Singh; design and technology is taught in the workshop by Mrs Evans, and so on. While the curriculum frameworks that have resulted in this division are understandable, it is important to remember that from a pupil's perspective this is a massive shift in how they experience the processes of teaching and learning in comparison to what they received throughout their primary education.

Generalist and specialist teachers

For a range of historical, societal and cultural reasons, and put simply, many primary school teachers are generalists, being able to teach many different subjects to their class throughout the week; secondary school teachers see themselves as subject specialists, teaching the same subject to multiple classes throughout the course of any given week. Although many primary school teachers may have a particular subject specialism (perhaps something that they have studied to degree level or beyond), the vast majority of them work in a generalist capacity. In some larger primary schools there may be subject specialist teachers but this is fairly uncommon.

The balance between an in-depth subject specialism and a more generalist approach to subject content can be both a strength and a weakness. Primary school teachers are experts in planning content from multiple subject areas in innovative combinations through sophisticated models of cross-curricular teaching and learning. For some primary school teachers, certain subjects may be perceived as being 'outside' their subject expertise and pedagogical comfort zone. When this feeling of unease becomes acute, it can even result in primary schools buying in curriculum support and delivery for that particular subject (thereby allowing the primary school teacher to pass that particular subject responsibility onto someone else).

The 'average' secondary school teacher is constrained by the notion of their 'subject' and how this is perceived and organized within the structure of the school and the various curriculum frameworks within which they work. At Key Stage 3, subject content is prescribed by the National Curriculum; as with the primary curriculum, the teaching of certain skills (e.g. the use of phonics to develop literacy skills) in specific ways will impact on their pedagogy (in helpful or unhelpful ways, depending on your point of view). At Key Stage 4, GCSE specifications will outline, in detail, exact areas of subject content that will need to be covered. The opportunity to devise innovative topic-based approaches within these structures could be seen to be limited (though we note that this does not stop some teachers innovating in these areas in spite of what some see as 'impositions' or 'restrictions' on their work; one example of this is explored in the second case study below).

Different notions of cross-curricularity

Linked to this point about generalist and specialist teachers, it is interesting to note that the idea of cross-curricularity within education is a highly contested and fraught area (Savage 2010). Even though every National Curriculum framework since 1992 has included statements that could be viewed as encouraging teachers to develop a broader, cross-curricular pedagogy, this has not happened within secondary schools. Teachers in these schools almost always view cross-curricular approaches to teaching and learning to mean working collaboratively with their colleagues on specific projects (perhaps within a collapsed timetable day). Unlike their primary colleagues who work with a natural cross-curricular disposition every day, many secondary school teachers have not been able to transpose what a cross-curricular approach might mean for their specific subject teaching.

For all these reasons, although there are several key areas of similarity, the broader processes of medium- and longer-term planning can differ between teachers in primary and secondary schools. In the following chapter, we will be exploring some of the documentation that these planning processes work within, as well as suggesting some particular planning documentation that you might like to use in your own work.

Here, what we would like to do is examine in a little more detail some of the consequences of the differences outlined above for the work of primary and secondary school teachers and, in particular we hope, attempt to bridge some of the differences and show how a greater understanding of how other teachers work can lead to a beneficial impact on one's own pedagogy. We will do this through two short case studies. The first is drawn from a primary school that we visited recently.

Case study 1: placing your pupils at the heart of your planning process

Effective teaching is facilitated through a professional relationship between the teacher and the pupil. How well you know your pupils individually will determine, to a large extent, the quality of the teaching that you are able to deliver. That said, teaching is not just about the delivery of 'stuff' to pupils. Pupils need to learn to know and trust their teachers too.

There are massive differences in scale here between primary and secondary schools. As we have already seen, in the average secondary school any one teacher may teach between 200 and 300 pupils every week; those same pupils are taught by between 10 and 15 different teachers. In the average primary school, one teacher may teach between 25 and 35 pupils and those same pupils may only be taught by that one teacher (perhaps with the support of another adult).

Given these basic numbers, and the consequent effect on the quality of teacher/pupil relationships that they might entail, is it really possible to place individual pupils at the heart of your planning process?

In our observations and discussions with primary school teachers, we were highly impressed by the constant focus on individual pupils, or small groups of two to three pupils, within their planning. In one teacher's work with a mixed Year 3 and 4 class, for example, guided and independent group activities were divided into different coloured groups. Within a weekly plan for the literacy activities surrounding the topic of 'explanation writing', these coloured groups were designed a range of differentiated activities within specific tasks. So, when exploring punctuation within this topic the teacher wrote:

> **Red: I can begin to use commas for pauses.**
> Provide children with copies of the comma text. Adult reads through first few sentences to model expressive reading using commas. Then, taking it in turns to read, the children read the text out loud and use the commas appropriately. Adult to stop children and re-read if they forget. Gussy and Finchy to focus on using full stops – write a simple sentence to go with the pictures from the ordering yesterday.

> **Green: I can use commas for 3 different reasons.**
> Provide children with copies of the commas sheet. They read the sentences out loud to a partner, making sure they are using the commas to help read them expressively. After that they label each of the sentences to show why the comma has been used, e.g. for lists, to break up longer sentences or to indicate additional information.

> **Purple: I can add further punctuation to sentences.**
> Children take the comma sentences and adapt and change them showing a full range of punctuation – can they add semi-colon, brackets, colon?

This kind of structured differentiation by task and, to a lesser extent in our observations, by outcome, was typical of how primary school teachers planned their work within a weekly cycle. However, as we explored in Chapter 3, approaches to differentiation are often more complex than just the breaking down of a task into different activities for different groups. In this teacher's work, as well as the task itself:

- the ways in which pupils were working with or without the teacher or classroom assistant were being differentiated;

- the resources available to pupils to help them complete their tasks were differentiated and tailored towards their particular activities;
- the learning objectives were structured in a differentiated way to ensure that all pupils had the opportunity to reflect on their progress using a simple self-assessment framework.

This whole episode from one teacher is situated with a way of working that really does place the individual child at the heart of the planning process. In conversation with that teacher, we were struck by the detailed knowledge she was able to articulate about every child in her class. Rigorous assessment processes can be conducted over a substantial period of time and can lead to a whole array of assessment data about individual pupils' work. However, the day-to-day human interactions that primary school teachers enjoy with their pupils provide a richer array of knowledge and understanding about what makes an individual child's learning 'tick'.

Secondary school teachers, in contrast, face the challenge of getting to know hundreds of children. While particular pupils might succeed academically within their curriculum area, and thereby become well known by particular teachers, the reality of teaching large numbers of pupils at Key Stages 3 and 4 are that these teachers will seldom develop the in-depth knowledge of individual pupils that their primary colleagues have been able to facilitate (despite the massive amounts of numerical data about pupil performance and attainment that schools generate).

In planning for the teaching of individual subjects in secondary schools (as we explored in Chapter 3), it is important to utilize a range of strategies for personalization and differentiation. However, our observations of teachers' work in this area have been that these are often more generalized and less focused on individual pupils. This is not a criticism. As we have argued here, it is a matter of scale and workload. We would not want to suggest that differentiation should result in individual lesson plans for every pupil! That is clearly ridiculous. However, there is a sense in which secondary school teachers can learn important lessons from their primary colleagues in this area.

Case study 2: exploring alternative approaches to planning for Key Stage 3

There are some writers and thinkers who think that the whole system of subjects being used as the building blocks for the curriculum is outdated and should be replaced. For example, Ken Robinson writes that:

> Education is the system that's supposed to develop our natural abilities and enable us to make our way in the world. Instead, it is stifling the

individual talents and abilities of too many students and killing their motivation to learn. . . . We need to eliminate the existing hierarchy of subjects. Elevating some disciplines over others only reinforces outmoded assumptions of industrialism and offends the principle of diversity. The arts, sciences, humanities, physical education, languages and maths all have equal and central contributions to make to a student's education. . . . The idea of separate subjects that have nothing in common offends the principle of dynamism. School systems should base their curriculum not on the idea of separate subjects, but on the much more fertile idea of disciplines . . . which makes possible a fluid and dynamic curriculum that is interdisciplinary.

(Sir Ken Robinson in Shepherd 2009)

We would not share this view. As we have argued throughout the book, whether you are a primary or secondary school teacher the notion of an individual academic subject plays an important part in framing how teaching and learning are structured. Subject cultures or traditions are important and powerful sets of ideas that frame our experiences in the wider world and, from our perspective, have a role to play in any educational provision.

However, we would agree with Robinson that there is an important job to do in re-imagining how subjects might be able to work together more constructively within education. In particular, the bridge between a pupil's experiences in primary school (where all subjects are taught predominantly by one teacher to one class) to secondary school (where each subject is taught individually to that pupil by different teachers) needs to be carefully constructed.

To that end, it is interesting to examine the work of secondary schools that have tried alternative arrangements to the provision of the curriculum, particularly in Year 7 (the first year of most secondary schooling). Some schools, albeit a significant minority, have thrown the whole concept of individual subjects out of the classroom window and rebuilt a curriculum around different organizatory structures. Perhaps the most famous example of this is the RSA's Opening Minds curriculum that is built around the five key competences of:

1 citizenship
2 learning
3 managing information
4 relating to people
5 managing situations

In the RSA's words, this approach:

> enables students not just to acquire subject knowledge but to understand, use and apply it within the context of their wider learning and

life. It also offers students a more holistic and coherent way of learning which allows them to make connections and apply knowledge across different subject areas.

(RSA 2013)

Despite comprehensive pieces of research and applied research by the RSA (Aynsley *et al.* 2012; Isham and Cordingley 2012), we are still uncertain that this is the most productive way forward.

One approach that we observed recently at a secondary school in Birmingham did seem particularly productive. This drew on a pedagogical approach known as 'the mantle of the expert'. It is defined as:

> a dramatic-inquiry based approach to teaching and learning invented and developed by Professor Dorothy Heathcote at the University of Newcastle upon Tyne in the 1980s. The big idea is that the class do all their curriculum work as if they are an imagined group of experts. They might be scientists in a laboratory or archaeologists excavating a tomb, or a rescue team at the scene of a disaster. They might be running a removal company, or a factory, or a shop, or a space station or a French resistance group. Because they behave 'as if they are experts', the children are working from a specific point of view as they explore their learning and this brings special responsibilities, language needs and social behaviours.
>
> (Mantle of the Expert 2013)

This pedagogical approach allows teachers to consider a number of areas simultaneously:

- Activity is social and collaborative; students work together negotiating meaning while sharing and deepening their understanding.
- It fuses pupils' capacity to be emotionally affected by a situation with their ability to reason about it.
- It requires inquiry into values as implications and consequences of action are scrutinized from inside a dilemma and from differing standpoints.
- It exploits the human capacity for liminality, so that pupils can be taught to tolerate ambiguity as they are on the threshold of new understandings that bring their own knowledge and experience into focus.
- It uses the critical dramatic elements of tension and constraint.
- It operates in the urgency of 'now' time. (Fautley *et al.* 2008: 107)

Our case study of this approach from the work of teachers at Queensbridge School in Birmingham (first published in Fautley and Savage 2011: 71–4) explored a particular example of Year 7 pupils working within a witness protection unit (WPU):

> *Here the learners were working at finding out what happens in a WPU, and then working through fictive situations as they evolved. In doing this, the students needed to investigate the communities where the suspects and witnesses lived. They needed to know about the community so that later, as WPU members, they could evaluate potential threats that might come from within it. This was a dialogic approach which added both breadth and depth to the fictional world within which the WPU episode took place. As a teacher involved observed:*
>
>> *They also played the gang members because we started to look at the gang and what it's like to be part of the gang. They played members of their families because we're looking at migration of people into Birmingham and a look at the generation gap between the gang members and their parents and grandparents. So they're having to look at ritual, religion and behaviour and manners and etiquette and all that kind of stuff . . . as WPU we're doing files on individual gang members . . . (using) drama to uncover key moments.*
>
> *This led to a wide range of activities and curricular coverage. For example, here is how one teacher described how aspects of the geography curriculum had been absorbed into the process, so that the knowledge, skills, and understandings involved all had coherence for the students:*
>
>> *They have done Google Earth and they went on the computer and they each had a satellite image, which is part of what they have to do with Geography, and then they had to locate the gang territory . . . find areas of ambush . . . look at land usage. It's all necessary for the fiction to continue. And then they would come and cross-reference with that map and do grid references and the next stage is, they can have groups, one of them is undercover and briefed outside and we found a new piece of evidence and they have to very quickly work out directions using that map in order for the undercover officer to get to Kelly's house before anything happens. So, again, there is a tension in that. So they're having to manipulate all the knowledge base in order to complete their jobs as WPU . . . we have to look at this in order to keep Kelly and her family safe . . . there is a need to know. The urgency is – she's in danger, right, so – who is on Taylor Road? Right – who's got the grid reference quick – so . . . you are all people in on it together rather than we (the teachers) are the people who know.*

This was with Year 7 students, and deals with subject matter which often would be considered to be the province of older students. What working within the convention of the mantle of the expert did was to allow teachers and students to delimit the areas which were appropriate to the pupils, while still stretching them.

One of the teachers involved spoke about student engagement with this process, where the students were co-constructors of their own learning:

> *. . . they love being in role as WPU (Witness Protection Unit), they love having the responsibility, they love seeing that they can influence the course of events. They love seeing that they have ownership of materials . . . whatever they do in one lesson is then fed into the next lesson. They love the freedom but also the discipline of it because, of course, it is very disciplined.*

To do this required a degree of flexibility from the teachers, and at times involved them responding to the learners, as this teacher observed:

> *Every lesson doesn't have to be totally prescriptive. We don't say, right, we're going to do this in this lesson, this is all we're going to do. You know if the pupils think of something that wants to take them off (my) track then we're quite confident and happy to do that.*

Working in this way has resonances with how topics are organized within the primary school curriculum. The specific pedagogical bridge that is being used here, the mantle of the expert, helped secondary school teachers reinterpret or re-imagine how subjects could both look and feel different for pupils when situated within a 'real-life' context (the WPU and associated elements). It is a very different way of thinking about how to construct learning opportunities that challenges conventional wisdom about how the curriculum should be organized.

This picks up on broader educational themes about curriculum development. As Bruner writes:

> Understanding consists in grasping the place of an idea or fact in some more general structure of knowledge . . . Acquired knowledge is most useful to a learner, moreover, when it is 'discovered' through the learner's own cognitive efforts, for it is then related to and used in reference to what one has known before. Such acts of discovery are enormously facilitated by the structure of knowledge itself, for however complicated any domain of knowledge may be, it can be

represented in ways that make it accessible through less complex elaborated processes. It was this conclusion that led me to propose that any subject could be taught to any child at any age in some form that was honest.

(Bruner 1996: xi–xii)

Summary: building bridges from primary to secondary

This chapter has explored some of the differences and tensions between planning learning within the primary and secondary schools. We have been at pains to ensure that we are not seen to be favouring one system above the other. They are just different. However, we do think that there is much to be gained by teachers within both systems sharing, at a deep level, aspects of their work in this area.

In our roles as initial teacher educators, researchers and writers we are in the privileged position of being able to routinely visit schools from each sector. Every week we watch student teachers and experienced colleagues working in schools, planning lessons, enacting these lessons and facilitating engagement that leads to learning and reflecting on these processes in different ways. Teaching in the primary school is not so different from teaching in the secondary school. However, the context is very different and this seriously impacts on how teachers do their jobs.

In your own work, try to find time to have regular conversations with teachers working in different school settings to your own. Share aspects of your pedagogy in this area and get their feedback. Be willing to try out new ideas and reflect on their effectiveness. Play with your pedagogy and be creative in how you bring new ideas to bear upon it. This is one way in which you can ensure a long and enjoyable career as a teacher.

Reflective questions

- How many pupils do you teach a week? Are there differences in your school? Who teaches the most?
- How are teaching and learning organized in your school? Are there any innovative ways new ideas are being tried?
- Do different subject areas in your school have different cultures?
- How much do you know about teaching and learning in schools and colleges in preceding and successive phases?

11 Lesson planning documentation

As we have observed throughout this book, there is no simple 'magic bullet' of a blank lesson planning document which will enable the teacher to plan for everything on every teaching and learning occasion, and which will also solve all imaginable class management issues, deal with behaviour problems, provide full differentiation, and only take a few moments to complete. Sorry!

What we will look at in this chapter is a variety of ways of setting out lesson planning documentation. There are many possible permutations for this, and it seems that every school has its own requirements, from the complex to the simple. We will try to pick our way through what is required and what is desirable, and will offer a number of suggestions.

One of the first things that it is important to say is to echo Sara Bubb's observation that 'spending excessive amounts of time on long, detailed plans does not necessarily lead to better teaching and learning' (2004 76). We have seen in Chapter 2 that beginning teachers tend to spend an inordinately long time on planning their lessons in the sincere expectation that by doing so they will 'plan out' all of the issues concerning behaviour management that could possibly occur. We repeat what we said then, that this is sadly not the case. However well planned a lesson is, it still has to be brought to life by the teacher. And as Sir Michael Wilshaw, Her Majesty's Chief Inspector of Education, has observed with regard to teachers he worked with:

> Planning was everything, but ... teachers were not slaves to their lesson plans. For each lesson, they would know what they were going to do, what resources they were going to deploy and roughly how long each activity would take. But they also understood that planning should not be too detailed or too rigid. It was a framework and support, but they adapted what they did at key moments in the lesson, for example when something was not working or when the mood of the class changed.
>
> (RSA 2012)

And this is an important message to bear in mind!

In this chapter we are not distinguishing significantly between age phases in terms of lesson planning. In previous chapters we have discussed differences and similarities between long- and medium-term planning for primary or secondary schools. In this chapter we think about the elements of a successful lesson, and what you, the teacher, need to do to enable this to happen. Clearly there will be some aspects which are phase-appropriate, but our concern here is with all learning, and we feel that individual teachers are best able to make their own judgements, and use the evidence we present to decide what is going to be most suitable for each individual context.

Linear or overview planning?

In this chapter there are examples of planning which follow a linear format, in other words, they plan out sequentially what should be taught and learned. Sometimes this is done using a timeline, where the number of minutes devoted to each activity is worked out in advance. We also present examples of what might be termed overview planning, where timing is not worked out in advance; instead planning takes on a more holistic form, concerning itself with the range and type of teaching and learning episodes that will occur, rather than strictly tying them down to a time-frame. There are no clear rules concerning this distinction, it is simply a matter of personal preference. We saw in Chapter 2 how novice teachers focus on the end of the lesson, whereas more experienced teachers focus back from the end. Some people like the idea of knowing what to do when; others prefer to be more holistic in their approach. What we would counsel against, though, is the problem we identify throughout this book, where teachers do not diverge from the lesson plan. If, say, ten minutes have been planned for activity A, and activity B is predicated upon successful completion of activity A, then there is no point finishing it after ten minutes just because the plan says so, even though the pupils have not yet mastered it sufficiently to progress! For beginning teachers, as we have discussed elsewhere in this book, 'running out of time' is a common problem, and so planning both an overview and a minute-by-minute account is going to be helpful for them. For more experienced teachers, the choice is likely to be dictated as much by school or other requirements, as by personal preference.

How much detail to include?

In Chapter 2 we discussed how it is the case that different degrees of information will be required at different times during a teacher's career, and for the different audiences for a lesson plan. Beginning teachers, and those in training,

PGCE Secondary
Lesson Plan – Notes for Guidance and Examples

Section A – Information

Subject:	Date:	Time of Lesson:	Duration of Lesson:
Unit of Work:	Class:	Number of Pupils:	Lesson number in unit:

Title/Focus of Lesson: A separate lesson plan should be completed for each class, even if the body of the lesson has been taught already to a different group

Section B – Professional Development Links:

The following **Teachers' Standards** (Prompts) will be addressed:
2 or 3 Teachers' Standards Prompts (sub-heading) is usual. Evidence from this lesson can be cross-referenced to the Professional Development Profile

Action Points from last lesson *(see section J of previous lesson plan)*: After the first lesson, this information ensures the sequential nature of lessons where learning is developmental

Section C – Aims: *Select aims related to the Unit of Work (maximum 2)*

To provide opportunities for pupils to:
Aims need to link clearly to those from the unit of work to which this lesson refers. They should be limited to those that **will be** addressed in **this lesson** rather than a list of those for the entire unit.

Section D – Intended Learning: By the end of the lesson... Differentiation for Groups: By the end of the lesson...

'**Groups**' (below) should be identified for this section and might include the gifted and talented (G&T), those with disabilities, Additional Learning Needs (ALN) or Special Educational Needs (SEN), Looked after children (LAC), English as an additional language (EAL), Free School Meals (FSM), Individual Education Plans (IEPs), Emotional and Behavioural Difficulties (EBD) and so on.

Pupils will have learned: Statements of intended learning should indicate what the majority of pupils in the group are expected to achieve, not do. It is helpful to use the stem '*pupils will have learned that or how to...*'	**Additional Challenge.** These pupils will have learned: Statements of intended learning in this section will be based on those to the left but will indicate additional learning challenges for the most able in the group.
Text to share with pupils related to intended learning: Where required, this text will be based on the intended learning statements but couched in pupil-friendly terms. The school's customs and requirements regarding intended learning can also be included here.	**Additional Support.** These pupils will have learned: Statements of intended learning in this section will be based on those above and left but will indicate learning for those in the group who require additional support.These pupils should also be appropriately challenged

Section E – Meeting Individual Needs: Briefly outline the measures you will take to meet the needs of some **named** pupils:

This section will indicate how **named** pupils will have access to the lesson in terms of activities, content, assumed skills and use of equipment. Clear and specific notes are expected to indicate the action the teacher will take to support these pupils. Across a sequence of lessons a

PGCE Secondary
Lesson Plan – Notes for Guidance and Examples

range of pupils should be considered, not only those with known or obvious needs. This section is very much concerned with **individuals**.

Section F - Resources Checklist: | Section G – Homework / Independent Learning:

A function list as an aide memoire	This shoud be in line with the school policy and should be linked clearly to the lesson. Success or assessment criteria should be included as well as tasks and logistical arrangements.

Section H - Lesson Plan:

Time:	Learning:	Teaching:	Assessment:
	The intended learning for each activity, with clear links or reference to Section D, above.	The teaching activities and strategies, and pupil activities. This should include key points/concepts for explanations and modelling, and key questions for questions and discussions. Detailing pupil activities separate from teacher activities will help to ensure that the balance of the lessons is in favour of pupils' learning. The relationship between the activities here, the learning (left) and the assessment (right) should be clear. Logistical arrangements for assessment activities should be included here.	Provide the criteria that will determine the success of the activity. This is important even where the response may seem obvious. Stating the intended response and/or outcome is important to clarify expectations.
For example	That Birmingham is an industrialised city	• Teacher models how to interrogate a picture using projection and writing key questions next to example picture; e.g. What does the picture show? Are there links between items? What are the implications of X, Y or Z? • Small groups interrogate pictures of B'ham City. Differentiated pictures used to scaffold responses and challenge the more able.	Pupils are able to identify buildings that pertain to industry and evidence of industrial activity. Most pupils draw conclusions beyond the picture – e.g. the canal was built to transport materials

BIRMINGHAM
CITY
University

Complete the following sections by hand as soon as possible after the lesson:

Class:	Date:	Time of Lesson:

Section I - Assessment for Learning

What have some individual [named] pupils learned in relation to your stated learning outcomes?	*What is the evidence for this?*
Section I (4 parts) must be completed after each lesson, the sooner the better. For this reason, handwriting the response is perfectly acceptable. Mere description of the lesson is inadequate here, as are bland statements such as *"the pupils achieved all of the intended learning.. "*. Responses need to reflect the extent to which intended learning was achieved the quality of learning. The **named** pupils should include those highlighted in Sections D and E above. For example: It was clear that Hassan understood that Birmingham is an industrialised city, making a number of connections between key features.	This section is a continuation and is intended to foster analysis, not merely description; it may be preferable to treat these two sections as one. Specific examples or instances from the lessons should be cited to clarify evaluative judgements made about named pupils. For example: This was evidence from the annotations made in connection with the picture. Hassan cited two good examples of synthesising information to arrive at conclusions.
What additional, unexpected or unplanned outcomes were apparent in this lesson?	*What learning targets for some individual pupils need to be set?*
References to enjoyment or behaviour are only significant in terms of how they affect achievement and progress. For example: Most pupils had not interrogated a picture in such a structured manner before. This appeared very successful.	The emphasis here is on learning targets rather than behavioural targets. For example: Hassan could be challenged by considering the Birmingham map of 1870. Anna describes well but needs to talk through implications of what she has indentified

Section J – Evidence of Reflective Practice: *Complete for every <u>lesson</u> taught until Easter. Complete for one lesson per day after Easter*

What aspects of the lesson were successful, and why?	*What are your action points for the next time you teach this group and/or lesson? (Transfer to the next lesson plan for this group/lesson)*
This needs to be objective and analytical; the what, how and why of the lesson. Strengths and achievements are also important and should be discussed. How pupils responded and reacted to the teaching might also be significant. For example: teacher modelling worked very well using IWB because the pupils saw the whole process and had a clear idea of expectations.	Identifying significant features must lead to strategies to change, develop or refine practice. Analysis must lead to action! For this reason, the requirement to complete this section is relaxed after Easter. For example: Include greater challenge for Hassan. Place Anna with Salema for guided talking activity.

© BCU School of Education/PGCE Secondary/Lesson Plan Guidance

Figure 11.1 University plan for PGCE secondary student teachers.

need to make their thinking obvious, so their lesson plans are likely to contain a great deal more by way of detail than those of teachers who have been in-post for a while. So, let us begin by considering the requirements of lesson planning for PGCE secondary students (see Figure 11.1).

This is a very complete lesson plan, with all the detail it would be expected that a trainee teacher would need to think about. This lesson plan has guidance provided to the students included, so that it is clear what is required.[1] It is worth deconstructing this document to think about what it is saying and what it is assuming. The information at the top of the form and the left of section B concerning the class and Teachers' Standards is clearly relevant to a beginning teacher, where the lesson plan serves a number of purposes, including monitoring (more on this later), and making planning visible to in-school mentors and others. The 'action points' section links to previous lesson plans. We have said before that planning needs to take account of what has gone before, and this section emphasizes that. 'Aims' refer specifically to this lesson, as would be expected. The 'intended learning' section includes a number of areas, but worthy of note is that there are intended learning statements which are for the benefit of the teacher, mentors and others in the school, and also space to express these in appropriate wording which will be shared with the pupils (this is a matter which we discussed in detail in Chapter 1). There are then sections on differentiation and meeting the needs of individual pupils. There then follow sections on Resources and Homework. Section H is a timeline for the lesson, with the various episodes and activities plotted out. Section I is a retrospective AfL question, where the beginning teacher reflects on the learning that has taken place, with a further more general reflection section to end with.

The Birmingham City University (BCU) plan is designed in part to render the thinking processes of the beginning teachers visible, and amenable to discussion with mentors and experienced teachers in school. This brings us back to the question we first asked in Chapter 2:

1   For whom is the lesson plan documentation intended?

We provided a range of answers to this. To this original question we can now add another:

2   What functions is it designed to serve?

These questions are not as naïve as they may first appear. The BCU plan is overtly designed in that part of its function is to hold beginning teachers to account for their planning. Teachers in the school, as well as placement tutors,

---

[1] Thanks to Simon Spencer of BCU for providing this example.

Timings	Activity	Differentiation	Resources needed
Starter			
Main			
Plenary			

Figure 11.2   Simple lesson plan blank.

will be asking questions concerning it, directed towards the beginning teacher. While this accountability is open and transparent in the case of a teacher in training, for more experienced teachers this accountability aspect of lesson planning may be less obvious, a point we return to later.

Moving to the other extreme from the university plan above, a much simpler lesson planning form is shown in reduced form (i.e. with blank spaces omitted[2]) in Figure 11.2. This is a very straightforward planning document which omits any extraneous matter and whose sole purpose is to allow the teacher to concentrate on planning the key aspects of learning activity which will take place during the course of the lesson. Another significant difference between this lesson plan outline and the one for the university students is that there is only a very limited potential for monitoring teacher performance here. The university plan is, as we have seen, deliberately detailed so that the thinking that goes into the planning is evidenced. The lesson plan in example 11.2 is not intended for this purpose. Any monitoring of the teacher here would need to take place in conversation and observation, not simply from the lesson planning documentation.

Other variations of this plan can also be found;[3] Figure 11.3 shows one such planning pro-forma. This is still a simple planning document, although slightly more complex than the previous example. It contains the essential features that the teacher will need to know in order to deliver the lesson, and enables straightforward activities and learning to take place for the whole class.

Another variation on the same theme is shown in Figure 11.4. This uses a slightly more graphical representation of the planning process, where differentiation and assessment are considered as impinging upon the learning episodes sequence of the main part of the lesson.

---

[2] This is the format adopted for other examples of planning documentation in this chapter – to save space, blank areas of planning pro-formas have been omitted.

[3] Including the popular '5-minute lesson plan' at *http://www.tes.co.uk/teaching-resource/The-5-Minute-Lesson-Plan-by-TeacherToolkit-6170564/*.

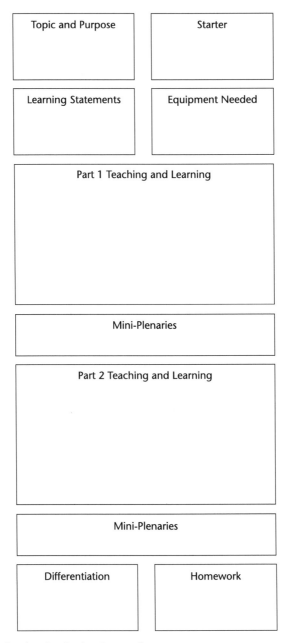

Figure 11.3 Another simple planning pro-forma.

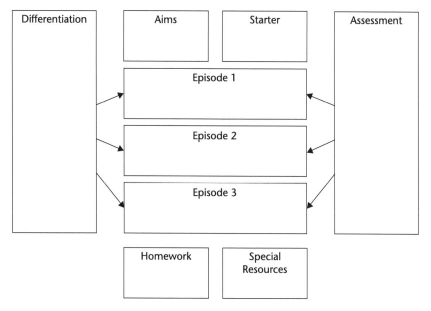

Figure 11.4 Slightly more complex planning.

In these days of accountability and performativity teachers are used to having their work scrutinized, and as a consequence are also used to the idea that their lesson plans will come under scrutiny. One consequence of this is that teachers have also become used to the idea that there will be differing levels of detail required in planning, depending not only on the purpose of the lesson, but also whether or not the lesson will be observed. This can affect the planning significantly, as knowing who the audience for a lesson plan will be is bound to have influence on thinking, planning and detail.

However, many schools are keen to elevate planning for teaching and learning to involve similar high degrees of forethought in much the same way as the university one did above. These should not be thought of being purposed solely to monitor teacher performance; the intention behind them is more complex than that. Such plans are designed to help teachers address key aspects of learning, to focus on personalizing learning for the actual class that will be taught, and to enable teachers to maximize opportunities for cohorts of pupils who warrant some form of differentiated provision. In and of itself this cannot be a bad thing; we hear too often about teachers teaching to a notional middle, which excludes many pupils not in this position. More complex planning can go some way towards addressing this. An example of such a plan used by schools in shown in Figure 11.5. Acronyms used in this lesson plan include:

Subject		Teacher		Other Adults in Class	
Date		Number of Pupils		Unit of Work	
Class		Period		Lesson number in UoW	

Learning Objectives(s)		Learning Outcomes		References to Exam Spec/National Curriculum	

Health & Safety Issues		Key Words	
SEN Students (Names)		SEN personalization	
G&T Students (Names)		G&T personalization	
EAL Students (Names)		EAL personalization	
LAC Students (Names)		LAC personalization	

In the boxes below, tick box if elements included in lesson. Refer to them specifically in planning

Literacy			Numeracy		PLTS	
Speaking		Understanding Texts	Measuring		Independent Enquirers	
Listening		Engaging and shaping text	Using number		Team Workers	
Group Talk		Organizing Text	Calculating		Creative Thinkers	
Coding		Writing in sentences	Shape		Self Managers	
Drama		Presentation	Using Data		Reflective Learners	
SPAG		Handwriting	Other maths skills		Effective Participators	

Curricular and Cross-Curricular Dimensions: tick box if elements included in lesson. Refer to them specifically in planning

Dimensions		Every Child Matters	
Community participation		Be Healthy	

Creativity and critical thinking		Stay Safe	
Enterprise		Enjoy and Achieve	
Global dimension and sustainable development		Make a Positive Contribution	
Healthy lifestyles		Achieve Economic Wellbeing	
Identity and cultural diversity			
Technology and the media			

Homework		Resources	

Element	Mins/Time	Teacher Work	Pupil Work	Assessment Opportunities
Starter				
Activity 1				
Mini-plenary				
Activity 2				
(Continue as necessary)				
Final Plenary				

Figure 11.5 A more complex lesson plan.

UoW = unit of work
SEN = special educational needs
G&T = gifted and talented
EAL = English as an additional language
LAC = looked after children
SPAG = spelling, punctuation and grammar
PLTS = personal learning and thinking skills

This is clearly a complex document, and requires the teacher to demonstrate their thinking in a very overt fashion. Although there is likely to be an element of monitoring involved in the use of this document, what is apparent, however, is that the use of the tick-boxes forces teachers to think about – and therefore plan for – aspects of the lesson as they apply to key groups of pupils, including SEN, G&T, EAL and LAC.

Planning for differentiation and personalization

Other lesson planning documentation used in schools involves a different approach to thinking about differentiation. One such example is shown in Figure 11.6.

This sort of lesson plan is designed for those schools where there is a need for careful thinking with regard to differentiation. We have discussed in earlier sections of this book that while it is the case that all classes can be considered to be of mixed ability in that they are made up of a number of individuals, it is going to be the case that some are more mixed than others! The purpose of Figure 11.6 is to highlight to the teacher while in the process of planning what range of the class's various needs and requirements should be included in the planning.

Another aspect of differentiation which needs to be considered here is that of personalization of planning. This can be looked at from two perspectives – the teacher's, and the pupil's. Let us start with the latter.

Differentiation needs to refer to the actual pupils in the class, where the learning needs to be personalized to meet their individual needs. In a number of the forms we look at in this chapter this is done by naming the pupils concerned. The EAL needs of pupils differs, as do their G&T needs, and so on. The planning for personalization should take account of this, and include real episodes for these named pupils to engage with. This is another reason why we are not generally in favour of having lesson plans written too far in advance of the lesson, as things change and sequential learning depends on what has gone before, which the teacher will only know about once it has happened.

Lesson Details			
Teacher	Subject	Date	Room
Class	Period		

Numbers of Learners			
Boys	Girls	EAL	G & T
School Action	School Action +	Statements	Support Staff present

Overview of learning experience	
Prior Lessons	
Next lesson	

Aims	
Learners will know	
Learners will understand	
Learners will be able to do	

Learning Outcomes	
Everyone will	
Most will	
Some more able will	

Assessment for Learning – I am going to use (describe)	
Peer Assessment	
Self Assessment	
Teacher Assessment	
Target Setting	
Assessed Task	
Spoken Feedback	
Written Feedback	
Questioning	
Other (describe)	

Differentiation – I am going to use (describe)	
Task	
Outcome	
Resources	
Questioning	
Time	
Difficulty	
Support	
Grouping	
Other (describe)	

Figure 11.6   Planning for differentiation.

Personalization of planning from the perspective of the teacher refers to the level of detail that needs to be included if the lesson plan is to be delivered by the person who planned it, or by another teacher. If the former, then the level of detail can be less than would be the case for the latter. Indeed, some teachers find it very difficult to teach someone else's lesson plan which they have not personalized in order to 'make it their own' beforehand.

Creativity

Creativity is generally thought to be a good thing in learners, and there are many aspects which you may want to include in your teaching and learning. One of the problems with creativity is that it is, by its very nature, non-linear. This means that if you want the pupils to engage in creative activities you need to plan for what you will do if they veer off at a tangent. This is going to depend on the nature of the topic and what learning you are wanting to take place. Planning for creativity entails not knowing fully in advance what will happen, but it also means ensuring you allow the pupils space and freedom for risk-taking, divergent thinking and unexpected outcomes. You may well want to include creative aspects in your planning, and these are clearly worth thinking about in advance.

Planning elements

From the examples so far discussed in this chapter, and from your own experiences as a teacher too, it is clear that there are many different approaches to lesson planning documentation. Among these a number of elements stand out as being common across lesson planning documents. These include those shown in Table 11.1. Although by no means exclusive, this does show a wide range of elements which can be included in a lesson plan. But which are the most important?; where does the real centre of planning thinking need to concentrate?

The three 'A's of planning

Although all aspects of planning for learning are important, three in particular seem to be ones which deserve the most attention, and should be at the centre of thinking about planning. These we refer to as the three As of planning:

- Aims
- Activities for learning
- Assessment (AfL and AofL)

Table 11.1 Common lesson planning documentation elements

Item	Meaning
Aims	The purpose of the lesson
Objectives	Places the aims into the specific learning context of the lesson
Starter	Activity at the beginning of a lesson
Plenary	Consolidating learning, often at the end of lesson
Mini-plenary	A plenary which happens during the course of the lesson
Differentiation (key cohorts: EAL, etc.)	How learning will be tailored to meet the needs of specific cohorts
Personalization	How learning will be tailored to meet the needs of the specific class, and named individuals within it
Teaching episodes	Division of the lesson into a planned sequence – teacher delivery
Learning episodes	Division of the lesson into a planned sequence – pupil activity
Activities	Learning-focused practical tasks
Learning organization	Whole class, groupwork, etc.
Teaching styles	Ways in which the teacher will deliver the lesson
Assessment (AofL; AfL)	How you will know whether, and how much, learning has taken place
Key words	For the lesson, or the pupils. Can be subject-specific or more general
Cross-curricular elements	Things which matter for the wider learning of the pupils
Literacy	Episodes relating to texts, even if obliquely
Numeracy	Episodes relating to numbers, counting, etc.
Speaking and listening	Pupil talk, turn-taking and understanding
ICT	How technology will be used
Creativity	Opportunities for divergent thinking
Resources	What equipment will be needed, physical and cognitive
Health and safety issues	These need planning for, and explaining to learners
Homework	What you will set, thought about in advance

Aims are clearly important. The answer to the 'why are we doing this, Miss?' question needs to be clear to the teacher, and the place of the lesson in the medium- and long-term schemes we have discussed earlier in this book should be an important part of what the teacher does, and why. The second A, **activities**, we are using in its broadest sense, and really mean the various *episodes* to teaching and learning which take place during the lesson. We are certainly not meaning activities to keep the pupils busy, we are referring to activities for *learning*.

Assessment is fundamental to learning. We have gone into considerable detail in earlier chapters concerning the vital role that AfL has to play, and it is this that should be central to both planning and delivery. One of the central messages in thinking about planning for learning is that however good the lesson plan is, it is how the teacher reacts to the actual learners in front of them that matters. Deviating from the plan is acceptable – indeed, a good teacher will know not only how and when to deviate, but also how to get back on track. This is true AfL in action. After all, as Wilshaw has observed: 'The worst lessons are those in which the teacher ploughs through the plan irrespective of how well or badly the lesson is going' (RSA 2012).

Of course, this does not mean that we are advocating ignoring all of the other aspects of lesson planning in favour of these, as clearly this would not result in good planning! Instead we are trying to focus in on those areas which can be seen as central to the process of lesson planning.

Build your own lesson plan document

For many teachers, school requirements of lesson planning documentation mean that there may be little scope to vary what is required. Where this is not the case, there is a lot to be said for teachers designing their own, either in departments, year teams or other organizational groups. There is also a case to be made for whole school planning to follow a common format. This means that managing teaching and learning across the whole school can be done using the same terminologies in different areas of schooling. It can also assist consistency across and between subjects, which is helpful both for pupils and teachers who teach in variety of teams. However, a point that does need to be borne in mind is that some whole school planning runs the danger of entailing too much extraneous or irrelevant work for some colleagues. It needs to be taken into consideration that some teachers teach 20 lessons a week to 20 different classes, whereas others teach 20 lessons a week to only five different classes. Each of these entails different planning parameters which a whole school plan needs to take into account if it is to address teaching and learning successfully.

Summary

We have looked in this chapter at a variety of types and formats of lesson planning documentation. We have considered a range of contents which lesson plans commonly entail, and we have looked at what simple lesson plans look like, as well as far more complex examples. We have journeyed to the very heart of lesson planning and considered the role that the three As of aims, activities and assessment can and should play in this. We have also thought about the important role of differentiation and personalization, and how the needs of the pupils in the class must be taken into account when planning.

Whatever type of documentation is chosen, what all of the different formats reinforce is another point we have been making throughout this book, namely that it is the thought that goes into constructing a lesson plan which is the important part. The resulting document is a product of thinking, it is not a short cut to it!

Reflective questions

- What planning documentation do you use?
- Why do you use it? If you have to, are there any aspects of it which do not suit you or your subject?
- If there are compulsory documents that you do have to use, how often are they reviewed?
- What would be on your own lesson planning proforma if you started with a blank page?

12 Conclusion

A book on lesson planning is rather like a set of instructions on how to plan an expedition. The points we have made during the course of the book will, hopefully, have shown you what you need to do in order to construct your own expedition into the exciting pinnacles of pedagogy! However, it is the expedition itself that is the important thing, and only in its undertaking will you know how successful the planning has been.

There are a great many things that need to be taken into consideration when teaching. We have been at great pains throughout this book to point out that planning for learning is an important part of a lesson, but that it is your skill in bringing that plan to life that will make for a compelling learning experience. After all, most of the pupils will be unaware that the lesson plan exists.

In drawing together the various threads that have run throughout this book, a number of themes seem to us to be of key importance. In among all of the deconstruction that we have undertaken, it is worth re-emphasizing some of these key themes.

Key themes

Teaching ≠ learning

There is no axiomatic linkage between what you teach, and what the pupils learn. They are not like USB memory sticks where you download your knowledge to them once and it stays like that forever. Learning is a much more complex process. A good teacher maximizes retention in their pupils, certainly, but they do this by making learning relevant, personalizing the content so it is suitable and appropriate for the classes they teach, and by teaching the content, knowledge, skills and understanding in a skilful way. But many pupils talk about more than this in successful teachers; they describe teachers who care.

Learning is more important than doing

Keeping pupils busy is easier than teaching them something. Most people can manage to keep a class occupied, but whether the pupils learn anything can be doubtful. Although completing tasks is important, certainly, it is not necessarily the same thing as learning. Planning for learning is harder than planning for doing, but is necessary for pupils to make progress.

The three As: aims, learning activities, assessment

Lessons which are of the 'turn to page 45, start copying out . . .' variety seem not to have any specific aims. What is the point? And that is why aims matter. Although a lot of time seems to be available to schooling, every minute counts. Aims should be statements that address the issues of, 'why this lesson, now, with these pupils?' This should be obvious to you, the teacher, because if it is not, how can it be clear to the pupils? Activities focused on learning are the core of a lesson so you will need to know what this involves. We have discussed a range of learning episodes and these need placing into a logical grouping and context so that your lesson can proceed according to plan. These activities will vary, will involve a range of types of learning, and will be purposefully designed with the classes you are teaching firmly in mind. Assessment will be key in this regard. The AfL judgements you make as you tweak your lesson plan while it is being taught, the conversations you have with pupils to see how they are getting on, and the reactions you get from the class as you try to develop understanding by careful questioning – all of these will make the difference between being a teacher and being a reflective teacher.

Your future development

We worry when we hear about teachers who feel they are complete and that they have nothing more to learn. The best teachers we have worked with are the opposite of this. They are the teachers who are always striving for better, who are interested in trying new ideas out, knowing that some will be useful and some not, they are teachers who reflect on what they do and what their pupils do. These are the teachers who make real differences in the classroom. These are the teachers we hope you aspire to be. We want you to be the best teacher you can be, and we believe that these are the teachers who will make a real difference to the young people in their charge.

This book has been written for teachers who are near the beginning of the journey from novice to expert, and we know that this journey takes time. We hope that the school, college or academy in which you teach supports you in this process, and we know too that it takes time to make this progression. There is an old saying to the effect of 'some people have ten years experience, others have one year's experience ten times'! In teaching, with its annual academic yearly cycle of terms, holidays, examinations and so on, it is easy for unreflective teachers to keep having the same one year of experience over and over again. Another key theme that has been running throughout this book is that of reflection, and this is an important component of moving annual experiences on to be cumulatively bigger than lots of multiples of one! We strongly recommend structured reflection and believe that this is all the more powerful if you can engage with others in doing it. The notion of having a 'critical friend' is an important one here, and schools which have established teacher research groups, either singly or collaboratively with others, have found that they reap significant benefits, as do the teachers who take part in them.

Finally, this book has been about lesson planning; as such we hope it is useful for that purpose, and that you are able to take some of the ideas set out here and put them into practice in your classroom. We hope too that you will continue to refer to it, even when you are far along the novice–expert trajectory, as it will then be down to you to help every succeeding generation of teachers in this regard.

Good luck, and good lesson planning!

References

Adams, J. (2013) *Hellmouth*. http://www.earbox.com/posts (accessed 13 May 2013).

Alexander, R.J. (2008) *Essays on Pedagogy*. London: Routledge.

Anderson, L.W., Krathwohl, D.R., Airasian, P. *et al.* (eds) (2001) *A Taxonomy for Learning, Teaching and Assessing: A Revision of Bloom's Taxonomy of Educational Objectives* (abridged edition). New York: Longman.

Aynsley, S., Brown, C. and Sebba, J. (2012) *Opening Minds: An Evaluative Literature Review*. London: RSA. Also available from http://www.thersa.org/__data/assets/pdf_file/0006/674889/RSAOMliteraturereview.pdf.

Bernstein, B. (1999) Official knowledge and pedagogic identities. In F. Christie (ed.) *Pedagogy and the Shaping of Consciousness*. London: Cassell, pp. 246–61.

Berry, A. (2008) *Tensions in Teaching about Teaching: Understanding Practice as a Teacher Educator*. Dordrecht: Springer.

Bloom, B.S. (1956) *Taxonomy of Educational Objectives, Handbook I: The Cognitive Domain*. New York: David McKay Co Inc.

Boaler, J., Wiliam, D. and Brown, M. (2000) Students' experiences of ability grouping: disaffection, polarisation and the construction of failure. *British Educational Research Journal*, 26(5): 631–48.

Brown, M. (2012) Traditional versus Progressive Education. In P. Adey and J. Dillon (eds) *Bad Education: Debunking Myths in Education*. Maidenhead: McGraw-Hill/Open University Press, pp. 95–109.

Bruner, J. (1996) *The Culture of Education*. Cambridge, MA: Harvard University Press.

Bubb, S. (2004) *The Insider's Guide to Early Professional Development – Succeed in Your First Five Years*. London: TES/RoutledgeFalmer.

Burton, D. (2003) Differentiation of schooling and pedagogy. In S. Bartlett and D. Burton (eds) *Education Studies: Essential Issues*. London: Sage, pp. 42–71.

Burton, D. (2005) Ways pupils learn. In S. Capel, M. Leask and T. Turner (eds) *Learning to Teach in the Secondary School: A Companion to School Experience*, 4th edn. London: Routledge, pp. 244–57.

Carr, N. (2010) *The Shallows: How the Internet is Changing the Way We Think, Read and Remember*. London: Atlantic Books.

Cate, C. (2005) *Friedrich Nietzsche*. New York: Overlook.

Cole, M. (1996) *Cultural Psychology: A Once and Future Discipline*. Cambridge, MA: Belknap Press of Harvard University.

Collins (2002) *Thesaurus of the English Language: Complete and Unabridged,* 2nd Edition. New York: HarperCollins.

Culkin, J. (1967) A schoolman's guide to Marshall McLuhan. *Saturday Review,* March 18.

DES (Department of Education and Science) (2013) *Music: Programme of Study.* http://www.education.gov.uk/schools/teachingandlearning/curriculum/secondary/b00199601/music (accessed 20 March 2013).

DEST (Australia's Department for Education, Science and Training) (2003) *Values Education Study. (Executive Summary Final Report).* Melbourne, Australia: Curriculum Corporation.

DfE (Department for Education) (2010) *Schools, Pupils and their Characteristics: January 2010.* http://www.education.gov.uk/researchandstatics/statistics/a00196394 (accessed 21 March 2013).

DfE (2011) *Reducing Bureaucracy in Schools: Lesson Planning.* http://www.education.gov.uk/schools/toolsandinitiatives/cuttingburdens/b0075738/reducing-bureaucracy/planning (accessed 15 May 2013).

DfE (2012) *Streamlining within English Comprehensive Schools.* http://education.gov.uk/aboutdfe/foi/disclosuresaboutschools/a0068565/streamlining-within-english-comprehensive-schools (accessed 10 November 2012).

DfEE (Department for Education and Employment) (1997) *Excellence in Schools.* London: Stationery Office.

DfES (2006) *2020 Vision – Report of the Teaching and Learning in 2020 Review Group.* Nottingham: DfES Publications.

DfES/QCA (Department for Education and Skills/Qualifications and Curriculum Authority) (2004) *Whole-school Development in Assessment for Learning: Unit 3 – Objective Led Lessons.* Norwich: HMSO.

Dobson, J. (2006) Taxi drivers' knowledge helps their brains grow. *The Independent,* 17 December.

Eliot, V. (ed.) (1988) *The Letters of T.S. Eliot 1989–1922,* Vol. 1. New York: Harcourt Brace Jovanovich.

Emden, C.J. (2005) *Nietzsche on Language, Consciousness and the Body.* Champaign: University of Illinois Press.

Engeström, Y. (1999) Activity theory and individual and social transformation. In Y. Engeström, R. Miettenen and R.L. Punamaki (eds) *Perspectives on Activity Theory.* Cambridge: Cambridge University Press, pp. 19–38.

Evans, R. (2013) Michael Gove's history curriculum is a pub quiz not an education. http://www.newstatesman.com/culture/culture/2013/03/michael-gove's-history-curriculum-pub-quiz-not-education (accessed 22 March 2013).

Fautley, M. (2010) *Assessment in Music Education.* Oxford: Oxford University Press.

Fautley, M., Gee, M., Hatcher, R. and Millard, E. (2008) *The Creative Partnerships Curriculum Projects at Kingstone School Barnsley and Queensbridge School Birmingham.* Birmingham: Birmingham City University.

Fautley, M. and Savage, J. (2007) *Creativity in Secondary Education*. Exeter: Learning Matters.

Fautley, M. and Savage, J. (2008) *Assessment for Learning and Teaching in Secondary Schools*. Exeter: Learning Matters.

Fautley, M. and Savage, J. (2011) *Cross-Curricular Teaching and Learning in the Secondary School: The Arts*. London: Routledge.

Gamoran, A. (2002) *Standards, Inequality and Ability Grouping in Schools*. http://www.ces.ed.ac.uk/PDF%20Files/Brief025.pdf (accessed 13 May 2013).

Garner, R. (2005) Humor, analogy and metaphor: H.A.M. it up in teaching. *Radical Pedagogy*, 6:2. Also available from http://radicalpedagogy.icaap.org/content/issue6_2/garner.html (accessed 14 January 2010).

Gibson, J. (1979) *The Ecological Approach to Visual Perception*. Boston, MA: Houghton Mifflin.

Goodson, I.F. and Mangen, J.M. (1997) Subject cultures and the introduction of classroom computers. In I.F. Goodson (ed.) *Subject Knowledge: Readings for the Study of School Subjects*. London: Falmer Press, pp. 105–21.

Green, S. and Bavelier, D. (2003) Action video game modifies visual selective attention. *Nature*, 423: 534–7.

Greenfield, P.M. (2009) Technology and informal education: what is taught, what is learned. *Science*, 323(5910): 69–71.

Harlen, W. (2005) Teachers' summative practices and assessment for learning – tensions and synergies. *The Curriculum Journal*, 16(2): 207–23.

Harlen, W. and James, M. (1997) Assessment and learning: differences and relationships between formative and summative assessments. *Assessment in Education*, 4(3): 365–79.

Hatcher, R. (1998) Labour, official school improvement and equality. *Journal of Education Policy*, 13(4): 485–99.

Hattie, J. (2009) *Visible Learning: A Synthesis of Over 800 Meta-analyses Related to Achievement*. New York: Routledge.

Henley, J. (2008) Learn as you play: Gloucestershire's adult ensembles from scratch. *National Association of Music Educators (NAME) Magazine*, 25: 31–5.

Hill, D. (1988) *Humor in the Classroom: A Handbook for Teachers*. Springfield, IL: Charles C. Thomas.

Ireson, J. and Hallam, S. (2001) *Ability Grouping in Education*. London: Paul Chapman.

Irons, A. (2007) *Enhancing Learning Through Formative Assessment and Feedback*. Abingdon: Routledge.

Isham, C. and Cordingley, P. (2012) *Opening Minds Action Research: Teaching, Learning and Assessment on Competence Based Programmes*. London: RSA. Also available from http://www.thersa.org/__data/assets/pdf_file/0012/1000740/RSAJ246_opening-minds_report_041212.ET.pdf (accessed 15 May 2013).

James, M. (2006) Assessment, teaching and theories of learning. In J. Gardner (ed.) *Assessment and Learning*. London: Sage, pp. 47–60.

James, M. and Brown, S. (2005) Grasping the TLRP nettle: preliminary analysis and some enduring issues surrounding the improvement of learning outcomes. *Curriculum Journal*, 16(1): 7–30.

James, M. and Lewis, J. (2012) Assessment in harmony with our understanding of learning: problems and possibilities. In J. Gardner (ed.) *Assessment and Learning*, 2nd edn. London, Sage, pp. 11–32.

Jephcote, M. and Davies, B. (2007) School subjects, subject communities and curriculum change: the social construction of economics in the school curriculum. *Cambridge Journal of Education*, 37(2): 207–27.

Jonassen, D.H., Tessmer, M. and Hannum, W.H. (1999) *Task Analysis Methods for Instructional Design*. Mahwah, NJ: Erlbaum Associates.

Kittler, F.A. (1999) *Gramophone, Film, Typewriter*. Stanford, CA: Stanford University Press.

Kushner, S. (1992) Section 5: Making observations. *The Arts, Education and Evaluation: An Introductory Pack with Practical Exercises*. Norwich: Centre for Applied Research in Education, University of East Anglia.

Lave, J. and Wenger, E. (1991) *Situated Learning: Legitimate Peripheral Participation*. Cambridge: Cambridge University Press.

Leask, M. and McCormick, J. (2009) Teaching styles. In S.A. Capel, M. Leask and T. Turner (eds) *Learning to Teach in the Secondary School: A Companion to School Experience*, 5th edn. London: Routledge, pp. 285–99.

Mantle of the Expert (2013) What is MOE? http://www.mantleoftheexpert.com/about-moe/introduction/what-is-moe/ (accessed 26 March 2013).

Mosston, M. and Ashworth, S. (2002) *Teaching Physical Education*, 5th edn. San Francisco, CA: B. Cummings.

Muijs, D. and Reynolds, D. (2005) *Effective Teaching: Evidence and Practice*, 2nd edn. London: Sage Publications.

Nardi, B. (1996) Studying context: a comparison of activity theory, situated action models and distributed cognition. In B. Nardi (ed.) *Context and Consciousness: Activity Theory and Human-computer Interaction*. Cambridge, MA: MIT Press, pp. 69–102.

Neesom, A. (2000) *Report on Teachers' Perceptions of Formative Assessment*. London: QCA.

Nyíri, J.C. (1994) Thinking with a word processor. In R. Casati (ed.) *Philosophy and the Cognitive Sciences*. Vienna: Hölder-Pichler-Tempsky, pp. 63–74.

Ofsted (2012) 'Outstanding teaching and learning in history in 100 minutes – Farlinghaye High School'. Good Practice Resource. http://www.ofsted.gov.uk/resources/good-practice-resource-outstanding-teaching-and-learning-history-100-minutes-farlinghaye-high-school (accessed 15 May 2013).

Paton, G. (2009) Adults 'abdicating responsibility' for children. http://www.telegraph.co.uk/education/6598138/Adults-abdicating-responsibility-for-children.html (accessed 10 December 2009).

Pirsig, R. (1974) *Zen and the Art of Motorcycle Maintenance*. London: Vintage.

Popkewitz, T. (1998) *Struggling for the Soul: The Politics of Schooling and the Construction of the Teacher*. New York: Teachers College Press.

Ramsden, P. (2003) *Learning to Teach in Higher Education*, 2nd edn. London: RoutledgeFalmer.

RSA (2012) http://www.thersa.org/fellowship/journal/archive/summer-2012/features/the-good-teacher (accessed 15 May 2013).

RSA (2013) *Opening minds*. http://www.thersa.org/action-research-centre/education/practical-projects/opening-minds (accessed 26 March 2013).

Ruddock, J. (ed.) (1995) *An Education that Empowers: A Collection of Lectures in Memory of Lawrence Stenhouse*. Clevedon: Multilingual Matters.

Ryle, G. (1949) *The Concept of Mind*. Harmondsworth: Penguin.

Sadler, D. (1989) Formative assessment and the design of instructional systems. *Instructional Science*, 18: 119–44.

Salter, J. (2005) Final word. *Report*, July/August. London: Association of Teachers and Lecturers.

Savage, J. (2005) Information communications technologies as a tool for re-imagining music education in the 21st century. *International Journal of Education & the Arts*, 6: 2. http://www.ijea.org/v6n2 (accessed 15 May 2013).

Savage, J. (2010) *Cross-curricular Teaching and Learning in the Secondary School*. London: Routledge.

Schön, D. (1983) *The Reflective Practitioner*. Aldershot: Academic Publishing.

Sfard, A. (1998) On two metaphors for learning and the dangers of choosing just one. *Educational Researcher*, 27(2): 4–13.

Shepherd, J. (2009) Fertile minds need feeding. http://www.guardian.co.uk/education/2009/feb/10/teaching-sats (accessed 20 March 2013).

Shulman, L. (1986) Those who understand: knowledge growth in teaching. *Educational Researcher*, 15(2): 4–14.

Silbeck, M. (1983) Lawrence Stenhouse: research methodology. *British Educational Research Journal*, 9(1): 11–20.

Sillence, E., Briggs, P., Harris, P. and Fishwick, L. (2007) How do patients evaluate and make use of online health information? *Social Science and Medicine*, 64(9): 1853–62.

Small, G. and Vorgan, G. (2008) *iBrain: Surviving the Technological Alteration of the Modern Mind*. New York: Collins.

Smith, C.M.M. and Sutherland, M.J. (2003) Setting or mixed ability? Teachers' views of the organisation of students for learning. *Journal of Research in Special Educational Needs*, 3(3): 141–6.

Sousa, D.A. (2001) *How the Brain Learns: A Classroom Teacher's Guide*, 2nd edn. Thousand Oaks, CA: Corwin Press.

Stenhouse, L. (1975) *An Introduction to Curriculum Research and Development*. London: Heinemann Educational.

Stenhouse, L. (1980) Product or process? A reply to Brian Crittenden, reprinted in J. Ruddock and D. Hopkins (eds) (1985) *Research as a Basis for Teaching.* London: Heinemann Educational.

Strauss, S. (2000) Theories of cognitive development and learning and their implications for curriculum development and teaching. In B. Moon, M. Ben-Peretz and S. Brown (eds) *Routledge International Companion to Education.* London: Routledge, pp. 28–50.

Swanwick, K. (1988) *Music, Mind and Education.* London: Routledge.

Swanwick, K. and Taylor, D. (1982) *Discovering Music.* London: Batsford.

TGAT (1988) *Task Group on Assessment and Testing: A Report.* London: DES.

Tomlinson, C.A. (2001) *How to Differentiate Instruction in Mixed-ability Classrooms.* Alexandria, VA: Association for Supervision & Curriculum Development.

Tomlinson, C.A. (2005) Grading and differentiation: paradox or good practice? *Theory into Practice*, 44(3): 262–9.

Torff, B. and Sternberg, R.J. (2001) *Understanding and Teaching the Intuitive Mind: Student and Teacher Learning.* Mahwah, NJ: Lawrence Erlbaum Associates.

Tulving, E. and Craik, F.I.M. (2000) *The Oxford Handbook of Memory.* Oxford: Oxford University Press.

Tunstall, P. and Gipps, C. (1996) Teacher feedback to young children in formative assessment. *British Educational Research Journal*, 22: 4.

Van Tassell-Baska, J. (1998) *Excellence in Educating Gifted and Talented Learners*, 3rd edn. Denver, Co: Love Publishing.

Vygotsky, L. (1978) *Mind in Society.* Cambridge, MA: Harvard University Press.

Vygotsky, L. (1987) Thinking and speech. In R.W. Rieber and A.S. Carton (eds) *The Collected Works of L.S. Vygotsky.* New York: Plenum, pp. 39–285.

Wiliam, D. (2008) Interview with Trude Slemmen, 16 June. http://www.dylan-wiliam.org/Dylan_Wiliams_website/Bios.html (accessed 15 May 2013).

Wood, D., Bruner, J. and Ross, G. (1976) The role of tutoring in problem solving. *Journal of Child Psychology and Psychiatry*, 17: 89–100.

Woollard, J. (2010) *Psychology for the Classroom: Behaviourism.* London: Routledge.

Zonal Marking (2012) England appoint Roy Hodgson. http://www.zonalmarking.net/2012/05/01/england-appoint-roy-hodgson/ (accessed 3 November 2012).

Index

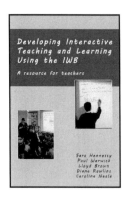

DEVELOPING INTERACTIVE TEACHING AND LEARNING USING THE IWB

Sara Hennessy and Paul Warwick

9780335263165 (Paperback)
October 2013

eBook also available

Interactive Whiteboards (IWBs) are now found in over 70% of UK classrooms (Futuresource Consulting, 2010). Yet research suggests that, at least in the initial years of use by teachers, they are used primarily to support pre-existing approaches to teaching and learning, rather than developing these in tandem with advancing technological expertise. It is also clear from research into classroom practices that, despite the need to develop interactive approaches that promote learning – in particular by engaging pupils in dialogue - evidence of the use of such approaches in classrooms is rare.

Key features:

- Using the IWB in tandem with advancing technological expertise
- To develop interactive approaches that promote learning
- Provide teachers with the rationale, model and examples they need to develop interactive approaches

 OPEN UNIVERSITY PRESS
McGraw - Hill Education

www.openup.co.uk

A-Z OF TEACHING

Jonathan Savage and Martin Fautley

9780335247004 (Paperback)
July 2013

eBook also available

This is an informative, engaging and accessible book about teaching that covers a broad range of content without being superficial. As suggested by the title, the structure will be alphabetical, covering a range of topics under each letter.

Key features:

- Practical teaching advice on areas such as questioning
- Each entry includes a short definition of the term
- Key ideas and key applications of the topic

www.openup.co.uk

 OPEN UNIVERSITY PRESS
McGraw - Hill Education

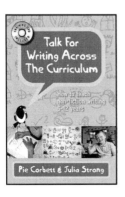

TALK FOR WRITING ACROSS THE CURRICULUM WITH DVD
How to Teach Non-fiction Writing 5-12 Years

Pie Corbett and Julia Strong

9780335240883 (Paperback)
2011

eBook also available

'Talk for Writing' is a proven approach to teaching creative writing that is fun, engaging and motivating for children. Now you can apply this approach to teaching non-fiction writing across the curriculum.

Talk for Writing across the Curriculum shows you how to help children speak the language of non-fiction before they attempt to write it. This is a three-step process using fun, multi-sensory activities. It helps build children's confidence and linguistic ability to such an extent they are able to create their own writing.

Key features:

- A wide range of fun, warm-up oral activities such as connective games, Professor Know-It-All, as well as text-based activities such as 'boxing up', creating toolkits and 'magpieing'
- Guidance for teachers on how to apply the approach across the curriculum
- DVD of Pie Corbett 's workshops with teachers showing 'Talk for Writing' in action

www.openup.co.uk

TOP TEACHER! GET IT RIGHT IN YOUR NQT YEAR

Neil Rutledge

9780335247240 (Paperback)
August 2014

eBook also available

This book chronologically mirrors a trainee teacher's path from seeking a post to progressing through their first year of employment and finally gaining their full QTS qualification. Each of the various challenges they must face along the way are considered, and advice and strategies given at each step are applicable to any ITE student or qualified teacher seeking to improve their practice. The style and approach of the book has been informed by focused interviews and discussions with around thirty recently qualified teachers; ITE students; and school mentors/ head teachers.

Key features:

- An anecdotal, non-academic approach grounded on research but also offers practical, easily accessible support
- Case studies and input from NQTs and recently qualified teachers, as well as perspectives from head teachers and school mentors
- A 'Get it Right!' theme with consequences flow charts allowing the reader to quickly appreciate the choices available and their consequences. Such charts are provided as a quick reference for all key content areas

www.openup.co.uk

TALK FOR WRITING IN SECONDARY SCHOOLS
How to Achieve Effective Reading, Writing and Communication Across the Curriculum, with DVD

Julia Strong

9780335262601 (Paperback)
August 2013

eBook also available

'*Talk for Writing*', developed by Pie Corbett supported by Julia Strong, is a proven approach to teaching writing that isengaging and motivating for students and teachers alike. Building on best practice, this practical guide takes you step by step through how to establish quality written communication across the secondary curriculum. It can be used as a handbook by a literacy coordinator to lead the approach as well as being a source of practical ideas for each subject area. Every teacher can help students internalize the pattern of language of their subject through focused talk activities related to exemplar text.

Key features:

- Wide range of examples from all subject areas with a particular focus on science
- DVD of a training session with teachers showing 'Talk for Writing' in action suitable to use on training days to help introduce and embed the approach
- Over 80 customisable handouts downloadable from the DVD

www.openup.co.uk